Slitting the Sycamore: Christ and Culture in the *New Evangelization*

Eduardo J. Echeverria

ACTON INSTITUTE

Christian Social Thought Series
Number 12 • Edited by Kevin Schmiesing

Christian Social Thought Series, Number 12

Cover Image: Riga, Latvia. © Jason Platt, 2007.
Image from istockphoto.com

ISSN 10 1-880595-28-1
ISSN 13 1-978-880595-28-1

Acton Institute
for the Study of Religion and Liberty

ACTON INSTITUTE

98 E. Fulton Street
Grand Rapids, Michigan 49503
Phone: 616-454-3080
Fax: 616-454-9454
www.acton.org

Printed in the United States of America

Contents

"True spirituality cannot be abstracted from truth at one end, nor from the whole man and the whole culture at the other. If there is a true spirituality, it must encompass all."[1]

—Francis A. Schaeffer

"The new evangelization that can make the twenty-first century a springtime of the Gospel is a task for the entire People of God, but will depend in a decisive way on the lay faithful being fully aware of their baptismal vocation and their responsibility for bringing the good news of Jesus Christ to their culture and society."[2]

—John Paul II

---

[1] Francis A. Schaeffer, *The God Who Is There*, 30th anniv. ed. (Downers Grove: InterVarsity Press, 1998), 177.

[2] John Paul II, *Springtime of Evangelization*, The Complete Texts of the Holy Father's 1998 ad Limina Addresses to the Bishops of the United States, ed. and intro. Fr. Thomas D. Williams, L.C. (San Francisco: Ignatius Press, 1999), 89.

Foreword

The volumes in this series on Christian social thought usually focus on discrete policy issues of contemporary interest, such as social security, intellectual property, and tort law reform. Occasionally, however, it is useful to withdraw from such policy debates and reexamine larger questions that lie behind those more specific issues. It is necessary to clarify the relevant theoretical framework before attempting to apply theory to practice. This is what volume 4 sought to accomplish with its treatment of the concept of justice, understanding of which is indispensably prior to any effort to ensure that political developments encourage the formation or maintenance of a just society.

The present volume, then, is another endeavor to clarify a sometimes confusing area of inquiry. Attempts by Christians to influence civic affairs are necessarily colored by the Church's and individuals' understandings of what is or should be the proper relationship between faith and public life, the Church and the world, Christ and culture. Eduardo Echeverria, learned in both the Reformed and Catholic theological traditions, illuminates the recent history of thought on this subject, and points to a way of thinking about the relationship that can appeal broadly to serious Christians in today's world.

Professor Echeverria rightly recognizes the seminal impact of H. Richard Niebuhr's taxonomy of the ways Christians view the relationship between Christ and culture. Yet, he uses

i

Niebuhr's schema as a starting point rather than as the definitive statement on the matter, at once adapting the categories and suggesting strengths and weaknesses among them—and evaluating all in light of the vision of Pope John Paul II's "new evangelization." Along the way, the author directs our attention to a suggestive image traced from the Book of Amos, through Basil of Cappadocia, to Pope Benedict XVI: the slitting of the sycamore tree (52).

Indeed, while recognizing the benefits and drawbacks of each of the approaches to the question, this series cannot pretend to be entirely neutral regarding the relation between Christianity and culture. Its purpose—to enlighten the thinking of Christians about how best to deal with certain issues of public importance—presupposes that Christians are called to engage the contemporary world at some level. Professor Echeverria shares that conviction and his analysis, deeply rooted in Scripture and Church teaching, furnishes guidance to all those striving to live genuinely Christian lives amid the social, economic, and political realities of their time.

Kevin Schmiesing
Acton Institute

1 Introduction

Integral Evangelization: Christ and Culture, Nature and Grace

Perhaps the most central theme in the almost twenty-seven-year pontificate of the late Pope John Paul II is the *call to the new evangelization*, that is, to the revitalization of the Christian faith at the heart of Western culture. This vital call for renewal is, in truth, an expression of the Church's missionary nature to preaching the gospel throughout the world, bringing the gospel to the whole spectrum of human life, and transforming creation from within and making it new—the plan of creation, fall, redemption, and the consummation of all creation in Christ. I believe that John Paul urged us to carry out the new evangelization as *integral evangelization*—to use a term of Aidan Nichols that nicely captures the full scope of this call.[3] As Nichols describes his understanding of integral evangelization, "I understand an evangelization that addresses all the dimensions of the person-in-society that Christian wisdom can help to flourish."[4] John Paul adds to this: "The men and women of today, like those of every time and place, are yearning for salvation. They wish *to rediscover the truth of God's dominion over creation and history, to encounter his*

---

[3] Fr. Aidan Nichols, O.P., "Integral Evangelization," *Josephinum Journal of Theology* 13, no. 1 (2006): 66–80.

[4] Nichols, "Integral Evangelization," 68.

self-revelation, and to experience his merciful love in all the dimensions of their lives. The great truth to be proclaimed to this and every age is that God has entered human history so that men and women can truly become children of God."[5] Furthermore, John Paul calls for a *new* evangelization, for integral evangelization, because Western culture has become missionary territory as it increasingly is more estranged from its Christian roots.[6] Moreover, the new evangelization includes not only a call to conversion, to respond to the gospel, but also to the renewal of contemporary civilization and culture, society, politics, and economics—indeed to the whole spectrum of life. John Paul was convinced that, as he put it, "A faith that does not become culture is a faith not fully accepted, not entirely thought out, not faithfully lived."[7]

In particular, integral evangelization includes, according to John Paul, *"a proclamation of the Church's social doctrine."* "There can be *no genuine solution of the 'social question,'* he adds, *"apart from the Gospel."*[8] That is,

> the Church's *social teaching* is itself a valid *instrument of evangelization.* As such, it proclaims God and his mystery of salvation in Christ to every human being, and for that very reason reveals man to himself. In this light, and only in this light, does it concern itself with everything else: the human rights of the individual, and in particular of the "working class," the family and education, the duties of the state, the ordering of national and international society, economic life, culture, war and peace, and respect for life from the moment of conception until death.[9]

---

[5] John Paul II, *Springtime of Evangelization*, 39.

[6] John Paul II, Apostolic Letter, November 10, 1994, *Tertio Millennio Adveniente*, no. 57.

[7] John Paul II, Letter instituting the Pontifical Council for Culture, May 20, 1982, AAS LXXIV (1982), 683–88, as cited in *Towards a Pastoral Approach to Culture*, Pontificial Council for Culture, 1999, no. 1.

[8] John Paul II, Encyclical Letter, May 1, 1991, *Centesimus Annus*, no. 5.

[9] John Paul II, *Centesimus Annus*, no. 54.

Now, one fundamental component of Catholic social teaching is the doctrine of natural law, which is a theonomic principle because it is grounded in the order of creation and, hence, of God's general moral revelation (cf. Rom. 2:13–15).[10] God is the source of this law, given to man in the very act of being created and in principle open to being known by human reason.[11] Significantly, natural law is essential to the evangelization of the power of the state. How so? Nichols explains,

> Evangelization of the State power means its confrontation with the abiding objectivity of the natural moral law, itself an expression of the divine Wisdom and the measure of all positive law on earth. Human beings govern—whether as law-makers or legislators, law-enforcers or rulers, or law-adjudicators or judges—only by participation in a higher law, by sharing in the care of divine providence for the common good, as by reference to moral truth people build characters that can fit them for life everlasting. No State is excused from the worship of God and obedience to a moral law both integral to that worship and the only stable foundation for human rights. Woe to that State that accepts the seduction of the serpent in the garden, "Ye shall be as gods," and seeks to establish the "natural measures of good and evil." The State's recognition of a higher norm—something implied in different ways in the founding documents of the American Republic and in the coronation of English monarchs—prepares the way for an acknowledgment of Christian

---

[10] On the relationship between natural law and general revelation, see J. Budziszewski, *Evangelicals in the Public Square* (Grand Rapids: Baker Academic, 2006), 15–37. See also, Russell Hittinger, *The First Grace: Rediscovering the Natural Law in a Post-Christian World* (Wilmington, Del.: ISI Books, 2003), esp. xi–xlvi, 3–37. For an important study of natural law in the Reformed tradition, see Stephen J. Grabill, *Rediscovering the Natural Law in Reformed Theological Ethics* (Grand Rapids: Eerdmans, 2006).

[11] For this definition of natural law, see *A Concise Dictionary of Theology*, ed. Gerald O'Collins, S.J. and Edward G. Farrugia, S.J. (New York: Paulist Press, 1991), 153.

> revelation, of which the coronation ceremony indeed
> is a quasi-sacramental expression. This brings us to
> the distinctively Christian aspect in the evangelization
> of civil society.[12]

In a latter part of this study, I shall consider briefly the contributions of John Paul II and Benedict XVI to the evangelization of civil society. For now, I want to make clear how it is that, in a Catholic theology of culture, the question of the relationship between nature, sin and grace—or among the orders of creation, fall into sin, redemption, and fulfillment—becomes the problem of faith and culture (and thus Christ and culture, Church and world).

At a recent national conference held at Sacred Heart Major Seminary on the new evangelization, the Archbishop of Chicago, Francis Cardinal George, who holds that the faith and culture relationship presupposes a truly Catholic theology of nature and grace, expressed the particular importance of this question.[13] He says, "Grace builds on nature, for human nature wounded by sin is not hopelessly corrupt. As grace builds on nature, so faith builds on culture, which is second nature. Culture is terribly damaged by human sinfulness, but seldom is it hopelessly corrupt. A culture is a field which offers plants from native seeds for grafting on to the tree of universal faith." "Faith transforms everything that is human," the Cardinal adds, "including culture."[14] In other words, as the

---

[12] Nichols, "Integral Evangelization," 76–77.

[13] Francis Cardinal George, "The Culture in Which We Evangelize" (paper presented at Sacred Heart Major Seminary, St. John Conference Center, Plymouth, Mich., March 24–26, 2006).

[14] For a more developed understanding of Cardinal George's views on the relationship of faith and culture, see "Catholic Faith and the Secular Academy," *Logos* 4, no. 4 (Fall 2001), 73–81; "One Lord and One Church for One World," *Origins* 30, no. 34 (February 8, 2001): 541, 543–49; "The Promotion of Missiological Studies in Seminaries," http://www.sedos.org/english/george_e.htm; "Law and Culture," *Ave Maria Law Review* 1, no. 1 (Spring 2003): 1–17; "A New Apologetics for a New Evangelization," *Theology Digest* 47, no.

French Catholic philosopher Jacques Maritain had already said in the first half of the last century, "the grace of the Incarnation draws to itself all that is human."[15]

Three quarters of a century past, Jacques Maritain significantly remarked regarding the question of the relationship of nature and grace that it is erroneous to ignore both the distinction between nature and grace as well as their union.[16]

Although Maritain firmly maintains the distinction between nature and grace, he nonetheless rejects a dualism of both a "hard" and a "soft" sort.[17] Hard dualism, which Maritain rejects, conceives of nature first in terms of its own end, to which is then "superadded" a second, supernatural end. Yet, Maritain also rejects a softer dualism in which a harmony between nature and grace is conceived, but there is still an *extrinsic* relationship between them. This more subtle form of dualism accepts that there is only one ultimate end for nature, a supernatural one, but it nonetheless fails to consider that this end directs and orders nature and all its intermediate ends, *from within* rather than alongside of or above nature.

---

4 (Winter 2000), 341–59; and "Public Morality in a Global Society: Catholics and Muslims in Dialogue," *Theology Digest* 49, no. 4 (Winter 2002): 319–33.

[15] Jacques Maritain, "The Conquest of Freedom," in *The Education of Man: The Educational Philosophy of Jacques Maritain*, ed. Donald and Idella Gallagher (Garden City, N.Y.: Doubleday, 1962), 159–79, and here at 179.

[16] Maritain states, "There is one error that consists in ignoring [the] distinction between nature and grace. There is another that consists in ignoring their union," *Clairvoyance de Rome* (Paris, 1929), 222. Cited in Henri de Lubac, "Apologetics and Theology," *Theological Fragments* (San Francisco: Ignatius Press, 1989), 91–104, and for this citation at 103n28. For an extensive discussion of Maritain's theology of nature and grace, see my essay, "Nature and Grace: The Theological Foundations of Jacques Maritain's Public Philosophy," *Journal of Markets & Morality* 4, no. 2 (2001): 240–68.

[17] For the conceptual distinction between hard and soft dualism, I am indebted to David L. Schindler, "Christology, Public Theology, and Thomism: de Lubac, Balthasar, and Murray," in *The Future of Thomism*, ed. Deal W. Hudson and Dennis William Moran (Minneapolis: American Maritain Association, 1992), 247–64.

By contrast to both forms of dualism, Maritain emphasizes that grace restores or transforms nature from within:

> It is clear that the order of redemption, or of the spiritual, or of the things that are God's, should vivify to its most intimate depths the order of terrestrial civilization, or of the temporal, or of the things that are Caesar's; but these two orders remain clearly distinct. They are distinct, [but] they are not separate. To abstract from Christianity, to put God and Christ aside when I work at the things of the world, to cut myself into two halves: A Christian half for the things of eternal life—and for the things of time, a pagan or diminished Christian, or ashamedly Christian, or neutral half…—such a splitting is only too frequent in practice.… In reality, the justice of the Gospel and the life of Christ within us want the whole of us, they want to take possession of everything, to impregnate all that we are and all that we do, in the secular as well as in the sacred. If grace takes hold of us and remakes us [in] the depths of our being, it is so that our whole action should feel its effects and be illuminated by it.[18]

For our purposes here, then, the *leitmotif* regarding a truly Catholic theology of the relationship of nature and grace can be formulated in the phrase: "grace restores or transforms nature." Now, this way of formulating the relationship between nature and grace will undoubtedly strike some neo-Calvinists such as Abraham Kuyper, Herman Bavinck, and Herman Dooyeweerd as decidedly un-Catholic.[19] For more than a century, neo-Calvinists have contrasted their own "organic way of relating nature and grace," as Bavinck puts it, with "the mechanical juxtaposition and dualistic worldview of the

---

[18] Jacques Maritain, *Integral Humanism: Temporal and Spiritual Problems of a New Christendom*, trans. Joseph Evans (1936; repr., New York: Scribner's, 1968), 292–93.

[19] Abraham Kuyper, *Lectures on Calvinism*, Stone Lectures (Grand Rapids: Eerdmans, 1931), 122–23.

Catholic Church."[20] On this "two-tier" relationship between nature and grace, they say, the latter is merely added (the *donum superadditim*) to a nature that has not been integrally affected by sin, and hence human nature requires little or no internal healing. I agree with Dooyeweerd that the mechanical juxtaposition and dualistic relationship of nature and grace is unquestionably found in both Protestant and Catholic traditions.[21] Furthermore, Catholic criticisms of this dualism have not been in short supply. Besides Etienne Gilson, they may also be found in the works of Karl Rahner, Henri de Lubac, Jacques Maritain, and Hans Urs von Balthasar, to name just several of the most illustrious but very different Catholic thinkers of the twentieth century.[22] Where I strongly disagree with Bavinck and, by implication with Dooyeweerd as well as Kuyper, is with the thesis that dualism is, in short, *the* defining view of the Catholic tradition over against the "ineluctable unity of nature, sin, and grace" (in the words of the American neo-Calvinist Henry Stob)[23] posited in the biblical revelation

---

[20] Herman Bavinck, *Reformed Dogmatics*, vol. 1: *Prolegomena*, ed. John Bolt, trans. John Vriend (1895; repr., Grand Rapids: Baker Academic, 2003), 303–5; 353–61. See also, Herman Bavinck, "Common Grace," trans. R. C. van Leeuwen, *Calvin Theological Journal* 24, no.1 (1989): 45–47, and for this quote, 60. "Common Grace" is a translation of Bavinck's rectorial address at Kampen Theological Seminary, Netherlands, in December 1894, entitled "De Algemeene Genade" (https://www.neocalvinisme.nl.hb/broch/hbag.html).

[21] Herman Dooyeweerd, *In the Twilight of Western Thought: Studies in the Pretended Autonomy of Philosophical Thought* (Nutley, N.J.: Craig Press, 1968), 44.

[22] Here is a sample of important criticisms of the nature-grace dualism from a Catholic standpoint. Henri De Lubac, *The Mystery of the Supernatural*, trans. Rosemary Sheed (1965; repr., New York: Crossroad, 1998). See also, De Lubac's *A Brief Catechesis on Nature and Grace*, trans. Richard Arnandez, F.S.C. (San Francisco: Ignatius Press, 1984); Karl Rahner, *Nature and Grace and Other Essays*, trans. Dinah Wharton (New York: Sheed and Ward, 1963); Hans Urs von Balthasar, *Love Alone* (New York: Sheed and Ward, 1969) and *The Theology of Karl Barth* (San Francisco: Ignatius Press, 1992); Maritain, *Integral Humanism*.

[23] Henry Stob, "Calvin and Aquinas," in *Theological Reflections: Essays on Related Themes* (Grand Rapids: Eerdmans, 1981), 126–30, and for this quote, 130. Stob shares the standard neo-Calvinist view that "Roman Catholic thinkers tend

and as grasped by neo-Calvinism. Although I, too, reject a "two-story" relationship between nature and grace, I share the view of Henri de Lubac, Jacques Maritain, Louis Dupre, Alasdair MacIntyre, Nicholas Wolterstorff, Arvin Vos, Dewey Hoitenga, and others that, to quote Calvinist Hoitenga: "This objection is directed against a later (sixteenth- and seventeenth-century) corruption within Catholic thought, which entered it under the spell of the new humanist, Cartesian, and later Enlightenment views of an autonomous conception of reason and will."[24] It would not be an exaggeration to say that this study of mine on the relationship of nature and grace, and the corresponding understanding of Christ and culture, is a defense of the thesis that the teaching of the Catholic Church on the biblical unity of nature, sin, and grace is remarkably similar to the teaching of the neo-Calvinist tradition.

I think that this is true not only in Maritain's case but also in that of John Paul II's. Indeed, this is how the late philosopher-pope describes the Church's mission of evangelization and, indeed, "the purpose of the Gospel," namely, "'to transform humanity from within and to make it new.' Like the yeast which leavens the whole measure of dough (cf. Matt. 13:33), the Gospel is meant to permeate all cultures and give them life from within, so that they may express the full truth about the human person and about human life."[25]

---

to regard created nature, both human and nonhuman, as integrally exempt from the ravages of sin, and to restrict the effect of sin to the loss of supernatural endowments (the *superadditum*) with which the human head of the created cosmos was originally engraced" ("Observations on the Concept of the Antithesis," in *Perspectives on the Christian Reformed Church: Studies in Its History, Theology, and Ecumenicity*, ed. Peter De Klerk and Richard R. De Ridder [Grand Rapids: Baker, 1983], 241–58).

24 Dewey J. Hoitenga, Jr., *John Calvin and the Will: A Critique and Corrective* (Grand Rapids: Baker, 1997), 113.

25 John Paul II, *Evangelium Vitae*, March 25, 1995 Encyclical Letter, no. 95. The quote within this quote is from Paul VI, 1975 Apostolic Exhortation, *Evangelii Nuntiandi*, no. 18. Paul VI adds, "The purpose of evangelization is therefore precisely this interior change, and if it had to be expressed in one sentence

This means that the redemption accomplished through Jesus Christ's saving work—his life, passion, death, resurrection, and ascension, in short, the Christ event—does not (1) stand opposed to, and hence replace altogether created reality because the latter is hopelessly corrupt as a consequence of the fall into sin. Nor does it merely (2) supplement or (3) parallel that reality, which would leave nature untouched by grace, and thus nature and grace would have only an *extrinsic* relationship to each other. Furthermore, nor does it merely involve (4) acceptance of created reality of one's humanity *as it is*, for that would deny created reality's fallen state, which would, as Fr. Thomas Guarino puts it, "overlook God's judgment on the world rendered dramatically in the cross of Christ."[26] Rather, reality stands in need of being reconsecrated to its Maker, and hence Christ's redemption (5) seeks to penetrate and restore *from within* the fallen order of creation,[27]

---

the best way of stating it would be to say that the Church evangelizes when she seeks to convert, solely through the divine power of the message she proclaims, both the personal and collective consciences of people, the activities in which they engage, and the lives and concrete milieu which are theirs."

[26] Thomas G. Guarino, *Foundations of Systematic Theology* (New York: T&T Clark, 2005), 20.

[27] I owe this succinct way of formulating the various possibilities of relating nature and grace to my friend and colleague Albert Wolters, "What Is To Be Done? Toward a Neo-Calvinist Agenda," at http://www.wrf.ca/comment/article.cfm?ID=142. Especially influential not only in my own thinking but also that of Wolter's on the relationship between nature and grace are the writings of Dutch neo-Calvinist philosopher Herman Dooyeweerd (1894–1977). For a brief introduction to his thinking, see *In the Twilight of Western Thought*. Also instructive is James M. Gustafson "Theological Bases," in *Protestant and Roman Catholic Ethics* (Chicago: University of Chicago Press, 1978), 95–37. On nature and grace in the early history of the Church, see Jaroslav Pelikan, "Nature and Grace," in *The Christian Tradition: A History of the Development of Doctrine*, vol. 1, *The Emergence of the Catholic Tradition* (100–600) (Chicago: University of Chicago Press, 1971), 278–331.

"bringing it to fullness of expression," as Francis Cardinal George says elsewhere.[28]

Against the background of the theology of nature and grace adumbrated above, I would like to revisit the enduring question of the relationship between Christ and culture. Deeply embedded in the Roman Catholic and Reformed traditions of historic Christianity is the conviction that Christians as such have a *normative cultural vocation* that God gave to man at creation. By exercising this vocation, man is realizing the design, or obeying the cultural mandate or commandment, given to him at creation to "Be fruitful and multiply, subdue the earth and have dominion over it" (Gen. 1:28).[29] As John Paul II explains in his last book: "These words are the earliest and most complete definition of human culture. To subdue and

---

[28] Regarding the relationship between faith and the world, Cardinal George asks, "What does the faith say to the world? To my mind, it says two things: first, the world is good, it was created good and therefore we are at home in it, and our faith is at home in it; second, the world is fallen. Because of sin, the world is estranged from God and therefore faith is something that makes us strangers in a strange land. These two questions and these two responses are both true, and people of faith live out their lives in the world in a dialectic between those two moments." Yet, there is more: "At the heart of the Incarnation, therefore, is God's loving embrace, in Christ, of the whole cosmos, that is to say the world of nature and the realm of human culture.... God's presence ... far from threatening or overwhelming the worldly, *raises it up and enhances it, bringing it to fullness of expression*" ("Catholic Faith and the Secular Academy," 75, 77, respectively; italics added).

[29] Both Catholic and Reformed thinkers regard this passage as the biblical warrant for the cultural mandate. On the Catholic tradition, see *Gaudium et Spes* (Pastoral Constitution on the Church in the Modern World), Vatican Council II, 7 December 1965, nos. 34, 57. Subsequent references to *Gaudium et Spes* (hereafter *GS*) will be made parenthetically in the text. See also the work of the great Italian-German Catholic priest, philosopher, and theologian, Romano Guardini (1885–1968) *The End of the Modern World* [*Das Ende der Neuzei*] (1950; repr., Wilmington, Del.: ISI Books, 2001). For the Reformed tradition, see Klaas Schilder, *Christ and Culture*, trans. G. van Rongen and W. Helder (1932; repr., Winnipeg: Premier, 1977), 37–41. For an insightful study of the Calvinist tradition on the enduring question, see Henry R. Van Til *The Calvinistic Concept of Culture* (1951; repr., Grand Rapids: Baker Academic, 2001).

have dominion over the earth means to discover and confirm the truth about being human.... To us and to our humanity, God has entrusted the visible world as a gift and also as a task. In other words, he has assigned us a particular mission: to accomplish the truth about ourselves and about the world." "We must be guided by the truth about ourselves," John Paul adds, "so as to be able to structure the visible world according to truth, correctly using it to serve our purposes, without abusing it. In other words, this twofold truth about the world and about ourselves provides the basis for every intervention by us upon creation."[30]

Although the foundation of this cultural mandate is in the order of creation, we must not lose sight of the basic truth that "cultures, like the people who give rise to them," says John Paul, "are marked by the 'mystery of evil' at work in human history."[31] Most importantly, still, "The good news of Christ continually renews the life and culture of fallen man" (*GS*, no. 58). This view "gives Christ, the Redeemer of man, center of the universe and of history, the scope of completely renewing the lives of men 'by opening the vast fields of culture to His saving power.'"[32] Moreover, from the Christian standpoint, this normative cultural vocation has eternal meaning and value and

---

[30] John Paul II, *Memory and Identity, Conversations at the Dawn of a Millennium* (New York: Rizzoli, 2005), 81.

[31] John Paul II, "Dialogue between Cultures for a Civilization of Love and Peace," *Origins* 30, no. 8 (January 4, 2001). See also, John Paul II, *Evangelium Vitae*, no. 104: "*life is always at the center of a great struggle* between good and evil, between light and darkness." Similarly, see *Centesimus Annus*, no. 25: "Through Christ's sacrifice on the Cross, the victory of the Kingdom of God has been achieved once and for all. Nevertheless," adds John Paul, "the Christian life involves a struggle against temptation and the forces of evil. Only at the end of history will the Lord return in glory for the final judgment (cf. *Mt* 25:31) with the establishment of a new heaven and a new earth (cf. 2 *PT* 3:13; *Rev* 21:1); but as long as time lasts the struggle between good and evil continues even in the human heart itself."

[32] *Towards a Pastoral Approach to Culture*, no. 6. The quote inside this quote is from John Paul II, *Homily of the Enthronement Mass*, October 22, 1978, *L'Osservatore Romano*.

hence is tied to eschatology because we will find the fruits of our labor, the subjection of the earth and mastery over it, "once again, cleansed this time from the stain of sin, illuminated and transfigured, when Christ presents to his Father an eternal and universal kingdom." "Here on earth the kingdom is mysteriously present; when the Lord comes it will enter into its perfection" (*GS*, no. 39). In short, culture, indeed all of fallen creation, belongs to God's culminating renewal in the kingdom of Jesus Christ.

In this book, I will develop an understanding of that vocation, drawing both on confessional Catholicism with its roots in the Augustinian and Thomist traditions and confessional Protestantism with its own roots in the Augustinian and more recent Reformed or neo-Calvinist tradition.[33] I write, however, primarily as a committed Roman Catholic who has been philosophically and theologically formed by both traditions. I am persuaded that the cross-fertilization of these great traditions has borne much fruit in my own reflections, not only on the relationship among *creation, fall into sin, redemption, and consummation/fulfillment*, as I have sketched these four basic Christian themes in the previous paragraph, but also on Tertullian's enduring question regarding the relationships between the gospel of Jesus Christ and cultures.

This book is organized as follows. In chapter 1, I shall expand in some depth on the indivisible unity of *creation, fall into sin, redemption, and consummation*. I follow this up in chapter 3 with five sections, each of which considers the following five typical answers to the enduring question of how Christ and

---

[33] By *Reformed* I mean that version of Protestant Christianity arising from the Calvinist Reformation in sixteenth-century Europe. The term *Neo-Calvinist* refers to a movement within Reformed Christianity that stems from the nineteenth-century Dutch educator, theologian, church leader, and politician Abraham Kuyper (1837–1920). Besides Kuyper, other genial spirits within this intellectual milieu include Herman Bavinck (1845–1921), Klaas Schilder (1890–1952), Gerritt C. Berkouwer (1904–1996), and Herman Dooyeweerd (1894–1977).

culture are related and whether the emphasis should be on *opposition* (Christ *against* culture) or *accommodation* (Christ *of* culture) or *fulfillment* (Christ *fulfiller* of culture) or *duality* (Christ *and* culture) or *transformation* (Christ the transformer of culture).[34] My aim is to describe such typical answers but also to argue that not one of these emphases by itself is sufficient in answering the enduring question. To that end, I will sketch, in a concluding chapter, the outline of a Catholic answer in which both Christ and culture are properly distinguished and affirmed in order to understand better the scope of John Paul II's call to the *new evangelization*.

---

[34] H. Richard Niebuhr's classic book, *Christ and Culture* (New York: Harper & Row, 1951), is the source of this typology of Christian answers to the enduring question of Christ and culture. I take my cue from Niebuhr's study of these types, but in general I do not follow his discussion of these types closely. Also helpful to me for a study of this question is Nicholas Wolterstorff, "Tertullian's Enduring Question," *The Cresset* (June/July 1999): 1–14.

II Theological Foundations: Creation/Fall/Redemption/ Consummation

God reveals himself in nature, history, culture, society, and human existence; indeed his omnipotence and wisdom; his goodness and justice; his blessings and judgments; and in short, his creation, maintenance, and governance embrace the totality of relationships within cosmic reality.[35] As the *Catechism of the Catholic Church* states, "The totality of what exists ... depends on the One who gives it being."[36] Yet, although creation is good and perfect in its own right, God did not make creation complete from the beginning. "The universe was created 'in a state of journeying' (*in statu viae*) toward an ultimate perfection yet to be attained, to which God has destined it. We call 'divine providence' the dispositions by which God guides his creation toward this perfection" (*CCC*, no. 302).

God is the sovereign Lord of creation, yet, he carries out his maintenance and governance of this creation in and through secondary causes, that is, "creatures' cooperation" (*CCC*, no. 306). In other words, "God grants his creatures not only their existence, but also the dignity of acting on their own, of being causes and principles for each other, and thus of cooperating in the accomplishment of his plan" (*CCC*, no. 306). Cultural

---

[35] Bavinck, *Reformed Dogmatics*, 1:310–11. G. C. Berkouwer, *General Revelation* (Grand Rapids: Eerdmans, 1955), 290–92.

[36] *Catechism of the Catholic Church*, no. 290. Subsequent references to the *Catechism* (hereafter *CCC*) will be made parenthetically in the text.

activity, then, which involves mastery, belongs to our very humanity, indeed our creatureliness, and because God operates in and through secondary causes, we are his coworkers, cooperating in his plan.

> To human beings God even gives the power of freely sharing in his providence by entrusting them with the responsibility of "subduing" the earth and having dominion over it. God thus enables men to be intelligent and free causes in order to complete the work of creation, to perfect its harmony for their own good and that of their neighbors. Though often unconscious collaborators with God's will, they can also enter deliberately into the divine plan by their actions, their prayers, and their sufferings. *They then fully become "God's fellow workers" and co-workers for his kingdom* (*CCC*, no. 307).

In particular, God has given man the mandate to be cultivator and custodian of the goods of creation, attaining mastery over nature, the social, and the cultural world; for example, establishing laws and legal institutions, developing science, the arts, family life, the whole civic community, and the free-market system. (cf. *GS*, nos. 53, 57).[37] Central to Catholic social teaching is the principle that in carrying out this mandate,

---

[37] See also, Wolterstorff, *Until Justice and Peace Embrace* (Grand Rapids: Eerdmans, 1983), 54–57. Herman Dooyeweerd explains admirably well the relationship among the cultural activity of attaining mastery over the natural world, social world, and oneself as well. He writes: "The cultural mode of formation reveals itself in two directions, which are closely connected with each other. On the one hand, it is a formative power over persons and unfolding itself by giving cultural form to their social existence; on the other, it appears as a controlling manner of shaping natural materials, things, or forces to cultural ends. The Germans speak of *Personkultur* and *Sachkultur*. Since all cultural phenomena are bound to human society in its historical development, the development of *Sachkultur* is in principle dependent on that of *Personkultur*. For the cultural formation of natural materials or forces can only occur by human persons, who must learn it by socio-cultural education, given in a socio-cultural form to their minds" (*In the Twilight of Western Thought*, 91–92).

man is perfecting the work of creation by bringing to fulfillment creation's potentialities for the sustenance of human life. Indeed, says John Paul II, "God gave the earth to the whole human race for the sustenance of all its members, without excluding or favoring anyone." He adds: "This is *the foundation of the universal destination of the earth's goods.*"[38] John Paul explains:

> The earth, by reason of its fruitfulness and its capacity to satisfy human needs, is God's first gift for the sustenance of human life. But the earth does not yield its fruits without a particular human response to God's gifts, that is to say, without work. It is through work that man using his intelligence and exercising his freedom, succeeds in dominating the earth and making it a fitting home. In this way, he makes part of the earth his own, precisely the part which he has acquired through work; this is *the origin of individual [private] property.* Obviously, he also has the responsibility not to hinder others from having their own part of God's gift; indeed, he must cooperate with others so that together all can dominate the earth.... This process, which throws practical light on a truth about the person which Christianity has constantly affirmed, should be viewed carefully and favorably. Indeed, besides the earth, man's principle resource is *man himself.* His intelligence enables him to discover the earth's productive potential and the many different ways in which human needs can be satisfied (*CA,* no. 31).[39]

Significantly, cultural activity, such as science, politics, and economics, cannot be considered only in the light of the order of creation because the influence of sin, of the presence and

---

[38] John Paul II, *Centesimus Annus,* no. 31. Subsequent references to this encyclical (hereafter *CA*) will be made parenthetically in the text.

[39] For a fuller treatment of the principle regarding the universal destination of the earth's goods and its relationship to private property, see *Compendium of the Social Doctrine of the Church,* Pontifical Council for Justice and Peace (Libreria Editrice Vaticana, 2004), 4.3.171–84.

universality of sin in man's history, in short, of the historic fall into sin central in the historical-redemptive narrative of Genesis 3, also manifests itself in such activity (cf. *CCC*, nos. 397–406). As Henri de Lubac once wrote, "No culture is really neutral."[40] I take de Lubac to mean that the world cannot be neutral with respect to the spiritual battle that is being waged in world history between the *Civitas Dei* and the *Civitas terrena*—to speak with Saint Augustine in a manner that is deeply biblical (cf. Eph. 6:10ff.).[41]

Indeed, if I understand John Paul II correctly, no cultural activity is neutral in that sense, not even the economic activity of the market economy. By the market economy, he means "an economic system which [rightly] recognizes the fundamental and positive role of business, the market, private property and the resulting responsibility for the means of production, as well as free human creativity in the economic sector" (*CA*, no. 42). This understanding of the market economy stands in contrast, he says, to an economic "system in which freedom

---

[40] De Lubac, *A Brief Catechesis on Nature and Grace*, 92.

[41] Jacques Maritain agrees. In his own words, the battle is between "*the World as the Antagonist*" and "*the World as redeemed and reconciled.*" He explains this antithesis admirably well: "The Gospel considers the world *in its concrete and existential connections with the Kingdom of God*, already present in our midst. The world cannot be neutral with respect to the Kingdom of God. Either it is vivified by it, or it struggles against it. In other words, the relation of the world with the universe of grace is either a relation of union and inclusion, or a relation of separation and conflict" (*On the Philosophy of History*, ed. Joseph W. Evans [New York: Scribner's, 1957], 133). On this, see also John Paul II's 1986 encyclical, *Dominum et Vivificantem*, "[T]he history of salvation shows that God's coming close and making himself present to man and the world, that marvelous 'condescension' of the Spirit, *meets with resistance and opposition* in our human reality.... Unfortunately, the resistance to the Holy Spirit which St. Paul emphasizes in the *interior and subjective dimension* as tension, struggle and rebellion taking place in the human heart [cf. Galatians 5:16–25], finds in every period of history and especially in the modern era its *external dimension*, which takes concrete form as the content of culture and civilization, as a *philosophical system*, an *ideology*, a *program* for action and for the shaping of human behavior" (nos. 55–56).

in the economic sector is not circumscribed within a strong juridical framework which places it at the service of human freedom in its totality, and which sees it as a particular aspect of that freedom, the core of which is ethical and religious" (*CA*, no. 42).[42] Of course, John Paul regards economic activity to be only "one dimension of the whole of human activity," and hence "economic freedom [to be] only one element of human freedom" (*CA*, no. 39). Thus, he opposes any view of the market economy that takes the economic aspect as absolute, in short, as man's highest good, taking it as the interpretative key for understanding the whole of reality, of man's social and cultural life. There are some serious consequences that follow from taking the economic aspect as absolute, according to John Paul II. This happens in the worldview of consumerism with its commercialization or commodification of the goods of human existence (cf. *CA*, nos. 36, 40–41).[43] For one thing, man is seen as nothing but a producer or consumer of goods rather than as a "subject who produces and consumes in order to live." Because the relationship between the human person and production or consumption of goods is, on this view, reversed, says John Paul, "economic freedom loses its necessary relationship to the human person and ends up by

---

[42] Of course John Paul II also rejects the Marxist socialist system, or what he also calls "State capitalism." "Marxism criticized capitalist bourgeois societies, blaming them for the commercialization and alienation of human existence. This rebuke is of course based on a mistaken and inadequate idea of alienation, derived solely from the sphere of relationships of production and ownership, that is, giving them a materialistic foundation and moreover denying the legitimacy and positive value of market relationships even in their own sphere. Marxism thus ends up by affirming that only in a collective society can alienation be eliminated." "The historical experience of socialist countries has," John Paul adds, "sadly demonstrated that collectivism does not do away with alienation but rather increases it, adding to it a lack of basic necessities and economic inefficiency" (*Centesimus Annus*, no. 41).

[43] For a critique of the worldview of consumerism, see Gregory R. Beabout and Eduardo J. Echeverria, "The Culture of Consumerism: A Catholic and Personalist Critique," *Journal of Markets & Morality* 5, no. 2 (Fall 2002): 339–83.

alienating and oppressing him." At the root of this reversal and, in consequence, self-alienation is a reductionist anthropology: reducing the totality of man's being to the sphere of economics and the satisfaction of material needs. Against this background, we can well understand John Paul's critical points that (1) an economic system as such does not possess criteria for distinguishing basic human needs ("real goods") from artificial needs ("apparent goods"), and (2) there are qualitative human needs and their corresponding goods that escape the logic of market mechanisms. Real human goods satisfy these human needs, says John Paul, and such goods "by their very nature cannot and must not be bought or sold" (*CA*, no. 40). Friendship, intimacy, human sexuality, community, love, pride, happiness, virtue, solidarity, health, human life, children, goodness, truth, knowledge, and last but not least, the reality and vocation of man's final end, namely, having been created by God and for God, man is called to share in the truth and highest good that is God himself—the nature of these goods is such that they are not and cannot be mere commodities.[44] When we make the economic aspect an absolute, we render the market an idol whereby the dignity and irreplaceable worth of the human person is undermined, given

---

[44] Of course the worldview of consumerism has left its mark on religion. As Craig M. Gay astutely notes, "The rise of denominational, and now religious, plurality in modern societies has led to a situation in which we are increasingly encouraged to 'shop for,' and so to be consumers of, religion itself. The consumption of religion, furthermore, suggests a fundamental change in the meaning of religious belief such that it has increasingly less to do with conviction [and truth] and more and more to do with personal preference. Many churches and religious organizations have responded to the changing meaning of belief by obligingly repackaging religion to make it conveniently and easily consumable. Such trends have contributed to the emergence of a kind of religious marketplace in which modern consumers are faced with a veritable smorgasbord of religious options" *The Complete Book of Everyday Christianity: An A-to-Z Guide to Following Christ in Every Aspect of Life*, ed. Robert Banks and R. Paul Stevens (Downers Grove: InterVarsity Press, 1997), 220–22, s.v. "Consumerism."

that human beings are treated as a commodity. The idolatry[45] of the market is one of the causes of man's self-alienation in contemporary culture.

> The concept of alienation needs to be led back to the Christian vision of reality, by recognizing in alienation a reversal of means and ends. When man does not recognize in himself and in others the value and grandeur of the human person, he effectively deprives himself of the possibility of benefiting from his humanity and of entering into that relationship of solidarity and communion with others for which God created him. Indeed, it is through the free gift of self that man truly finds himself. This gift is made possible by the human person's essential 'capacity for transcendence'.... As a person, he can give himself to another person or to other persons, and ultimately to God, who is the author of his being and who alone can fully accept his gift. A man is alienated if he refuses to transcend himself and to live the experience of self-giving and of the formation of an authentic human community oriented towards his final destiny, which is God. A society is alienated if its forms of social organization, production and consumption make it more difficult to offer this gift of self and to establish this solidarity between people (*CA*, no. 41).

John Paul II's analysis of consumerism brings us back to the religious dynamics of our culture. In sum, then, "A monumental struggle [of the Kingdom of God] against the powers of evil pervades the whole history of man" (*GS*, no. 37). Thus,

---

[45] On idolatry, see the *Catechism of the Catholic Church*, "Idolatry not only refers to false pagan worship. It remains a constant temptation to faith. Idolatry consists in divinizing what is not God. Man commits idolatry whenever he honors and reveres a creature in place of God, whether this be gods or demons (e.g., Satanism), power, pleasure, race, ancestors, the State, money, et cetera. Jesus says, 'You cannot serve God and mammon' [Matthew 6:24].... Idolatry rejects the unique Lordship of God; it is therefore incompatible with communion with God" (no. 2113).

the drama of man's life is a spiritual battle throughout the whole of the temporal creation (cf. *CCC*, no. 409). "Finding himself in the midst of the battlefield man has to struggle to do what is right, and it is at great cost to himself, and aided by God's grace, that he succeeds in achieving his own inner integrity. Hence, the church of Christ, trusting in the design of the creator (to be cultivator and custodian of the goods of creation) and admitting that progress can contribute to man's true happiness, still feels called upon to echo the words of the apostle: 'Do not be conformed to this world' (Rom. 12:2)." "'World' here means," the Council Fathers add, "a spirit of vanity and malice whereby human activity from being ordered to the service of God and man is distorted to an instrument of sin" (*GS*, no. 37).

This means, in particular, that Christians may not embrace an *optimistic* view of cultural progress. Alternatively, they may not embrace the radical *pessimism* entailed by the cultural judgment that our culture is *slouching toward Gomorrah* (read: cultural decline), or, as Herman Dooyeweerd has put it, "resign to an abandonment of culture to the power of apostasy." "In the light of the Christian basic motive of Redemption," adds Dooyeweerd, "culture belongs to the Kingdom of Jesus Christ. And the task set to mankind in the cultural commandment of creation should be fulfilled in a continuous contest with the historical development of the power of sin, a contest to be waged through the spiritual power of the Redeemer."[46] This spiritual power has its source in the finished work of Jesus Christ the Redeemer, the Incarnate Word, the Eternal Son of God become man—his life, passion, death on the cross, bodily resurrection from the dead, and ascension into heaven—and renews the life and culture of fallen man. "It combats and removes the error and evil which flow from the ever-present

---

[46] Herman Dooyeweerd, *A New Critique of Theoretical Thought*, trans. David H. Freeman and H. de Jongste (1936; repr., Philadelphia: Presbyterian & Reformed, 1955), 2:262.

attraction of sin. It never ceases to purify and elevate the morality of peoples. It takes the spiritual qualities and endowments of every age and nation, and with supernatural riches it causes [man's life and culture] to blossom, as it were, *from within; it fortifies, completes and restores them in Christ*" (*GS*, no. 58; italics added).

This evangelical Catholic and reforming view of culture is, as Nicholas Wolterstorff rightly says, "gripped by the Colossian's vision of cosmic redemption."[47] Basic to this vision is the truth that *the whole creation is recapitulated in Christ* (*GS*, no. 38). In the written Word of God, the lordship of Jesus Christ over creation and redemption is revealed (Phil. 2:11). Thus, "The Lord is the goal of human history, the focal point of the desires of history and civilization, the center of mankind, the joy of all hearts, and the fulfillment of all aspirations" (*GS*, no. 45). It follows from this vision of cosmic redemption that Christians are called to engage in the sanctification of culture by transforming it through God's grace in Christ. In short, they are called to the work of restoring all areas of culture, indeed, all dimensions of human existence, all of creation itself, to Christ, so that "in everything he might be preeminent" (Col. 1:18), and of making them share in the redemption he accomplished,

---

[47] On this, see Wolterstorff's "Keeping Faith: Talks for the New Faculty at Calvin College," *Occasional Papers from Calvin College* 7, no. 1 (February 1989): 13. See also John Paul II's 1986 encyclical, *Dominum et Vivificantem* "The Incarnation of God the Son signifies the taking up into unity with God not only of human nature, but in *this human nature, in a sense, of everything that is 'flesh'*: the whole of humanity, the entire visible and material world. The Incarnation, then, also has a cosmic significance, a cosmic dimension. The 'first-born of all creation,' becoming incarnate in the individual humanity of Christ, unites himself in some way with the entire reality of man, which is also 'flesh,' and in this reality with all 'flesh,' with the whole of creation.... He who in the mystery of creation *gives life* to man and the cosmos in its many different forms, visible and invisible, again *renews* this life through the mystery of the Incarnation. Creation is thus completed by the Incarnation and since that moment is permeated by the powers of the Redemption, powers which fill humanity and all creation" (nos. 50, 52).

and in this way to be his agents, coworkers, for exercising his lordship in creation.[48]

As the Pontifical Council for Culture states in a passage I cited above: "[A] Christian cultural project … gives Christ, the Redeemer of man, center of the universe and of history, the scope of completely renewing the lives of men 'by opening the vast fields of culture to His saving power.'"[49] In sum, the Pontifical Council explains, "the primary objective of [this] approach to culture is to inject the lifeblood of the Gospel into cultures to renew from within and transform in the light of Revelation the visions of men and society that shape cultures, the concepts of men and women, of the family and of education, of school and of university, of freedom and of truth, of labor and of leisure, of the economy and of society, of the sciences and of the arts."[50]

God created everything good, but this whole creation has suffered the radical fall into sin. Requiring divine recreation, renewal, and restoration, creation is thus redeemed in Jesus Christ, made a new creation at its very root, and "is in principle again directed toward God and thereby wrested free from the power of Satan."[51] God continues, even now, until the return of Christ, to work for the consummation of his plan in the renewal of the entire creation. In this restoration, we are his coworkers, agents in the struggle that God's kingdom continues to wage against the kingdom of darkness until his consummating total recreation—the new heavens and the new earth (cf. Rev. 21:1–4). "The good things—such as human dignity, brotherhood and freedom, all the good fruits of nature and of human enterprise—that in the Lord's Spirit and according to

---

[48] On this, see *Lumen Gentium* [Dogmatic Constitution on the Church], Second Vatican Council, November 21, 1964, nos. 30–38, 57–59; and also *Apostolicam Actuositatem* [Decree on the Apostolate of Lay People], November 18, 1965, especially nos. 5–7.

[49] *Towards a Pastoral Approach to Culture*, nos. 3, 6.

[50] *Towards a Pastoral Approach to Culture*, no. 25.

[51] Dooyeweerd, *A New Critique of Theoretical Thought*, 1:175.

his command have spread throughout the earth, having been purified of every stain [of sin], illuminated and transfigured, belong to the Kingdom of truth and life, of holiness and grace, of justice, of love and of peace that Christ will present to the father, and *it is there that we shall once again find them* (italics added)."[52] Not only is culture, then, eschatologically oriented, but also the whole creation ever looks forward to its consummation in Christ: "to unite all things in him, things in heaven and things on earth" (Eph. 1:10).

---

[52] *Compendium of the Social Doctrine of the Church*, no. 57.

III Toward a Theology of Christ and Culture

Christ *Against* Culture

Is life in this world *only* a means of reaching the end of forever enjoying God in heaven? If so, then life here and now seemingly would have merely instrumental value, extrinsic to the Christian life, rather than essential to living that life in Jesus Christ. Of course, what is right about this view is that communion with God is the supreme good and that the cultivation and enjoyment of all created human goods should be pursued in a rightly ordered relationship with God. Pushed to the extreme, however, this view may encourage us to think of life here and now as a mere waiting room with "the only task that [does] matter [being] the contemplation of heavenly things." "Only the making of a soul [is] the true human value," adds John Courtney Murray. "For the rest, what [does] it matter whether one [weaves] baskets or wrought[s] whole civilizations?"[53] Put differently, this view may encourage us to think of participating in the life of culture as a necessary evil rather than as a normative cultural vocation essential to serving God.

Furthermore, this conclusion has led some Christians to the view that the *natural realm*, that is, the created world, society, history, indeed the entire human cultural enterprise—the

---

[53] John Courtney Murray, S.J., *We Hold These Truths: Catholic Reflections on the American Proposition* (New York: Sheed and Ward, 1960), esp. 175–96, and for these quotes, 187.

cultivation of, for example, the arts, sciences, laws, and juridical institutions—is radically corrupt, evil, threatening, or inferior such that, as Christians, we must turn away from it toward an entire *otherworldly*, *supernatural* goal.[54] Abraham Kuyper rightly rejects this view, which posits an antithesis between the Christian faith and the created world. He writes,

> The world after the fall is no lost planet, only destined now to afford the Church a place in which to continue her combats; and humanity is no aimless mass of people which only serves the purpose of giving birth to the elect. On the contrary, the world now, as well as in the beginning, is the theater for the mighty works of God, and humanity remains a creation of His hand, which, apart, from salvation, completes under this present dispensation, here on earth a mighty process, and in its historical development is to glorify the name of Almighty God.[55]

---

[54] I am indebted to German Grisez for this way of posing the sacred-secular, supernatural-natural, grace-nature problematic. On this, see his master work, *The Way of the Lord Jesus*, vol. 1, *Christian Moral Principles* (Chicago: Franciscan Herald Press, 1983), 16–17, 807–30, and for this citation at 811. Also helpful to me was Wolterstorff, *Until Justice and Peace Embrace*, 3–22.

[55] Kuyper, *Lectures on Calvinism*, 162. This, too, is the view of John Henry Cardinal Newman in his famous autobiography, *Apologia Pro Vita Sua* (1864; repr., New York: Random House, 1950). The Catholic Church

> does not teach that human nature is irreclaimable, else wherefore should she be sent? Not that it is to be shattered and reversed, but to be extricated, purified, and restored; not that it is a mere mass of evil, but that it has the promise of great things, and even now has a virtue and a praise proper to itself. But in the next place she knows and she preaches that such a restoration, as she aims at effecting in it, must be brought about, not simply through any outward provision of preaching and teaching, even though it be her own, but from a certain inward spiritual power or grace imparted directly from above, and which is in her keeping. She has it in charge to rescue human nature from its misery, but not simply by raising it upon its own level, but by lifting it up to a higher level than its own." (245)

No doubt, this view threatens not only the Christian belief in the inherent goodness of creation, devaluing all the this-worldly goods of the human enterprise but also the radical and integral nature of redemption in Jesus Christ through which the entire fallen creation is renewed, including a Christian transformation of culture.[56] Put differently, the Christ *against* culture view has led some Christians—both Protestant and Catholic—to accept a false dichotomy within the Christian life between the sacred and secular, the supernatural and merely natural, and grace and nature. Ironically, this contempt for the world that stems from *opposing* Christ and culture, which results in withdrawing from the world and its corollary, a "citadel mentality,"[57] also has the unintended consequence of fostering the "wholesale secularization of culture."[58] Maritain

---

[56] Pushed to the extreme, the supporters of the Christ against culture position convert the spiritual dualism "into an ontological bifurcation of reality." Their rejection of culture leads to "the problem of the relation of Jesus Christ to the Creator of nature and Governor of history ... ultimately they are tempted to divide the world into the material realm governed by a principle opposed to Christ and a spiritual realm guided by the spiritual God" (Niebuhr, *Christ and Culture*, 80–81).

[57] By citadel mentality I mean, as Schaeffer put it more than thirty years ago: "living in a castle with the drawbridge up and occasionally tossing a stone over the walls ... [A] Citadel mentality—sitting inside [the castle] and saying, 'You cannot reach me here'" (*The God Who Is There*, 172).

[58] Tracey Rowland, *Culture and the Thomist Tradition After Vatican II* (New York: Routledge, 2003), 29. Regarding the dualism between nature and grace and its implication of "total secularization," see De Lubac, *The Mystery of the Supernatural*, 35. See also, Henri De Lubac, *Catholicism: Christ and the Common Destiny of Man*, trans. Lancelot C. Sheppard and Sister Elizabeth Englund, O.C.D. (1938; repr., San Francisco: Ignatius Press, 1988), 313–14:

> the supernatural, deprived of its organic links with nature, tended to be understood by some as a mere "super-nature," a "double" of nature. Furthermore, after such a complete separation what misgivings could the supernatural cause to naturalism? ... Such a dualism, just when it imagined that it was most successfully opposing the negations of naturalism, was most strongly influenced by it, and the transcendence in which it hoped to preserve the supernatural with such jealous care was, in fact, a banishment. The most confirmed secularists found in it, in spite of itself, an ally.

rightly traces this consequence back to an incorrect theology of nature and grace. He writes: "[A]s a result of the achievement of grace, as a result of grace [penetrating and] perfecting [and transforming] nature, nature is superelevated in its own order.... If we do not admit it, we are led willy-nilly to a kind of separatism between nature and grace, to a kind of naturalism—nature will have its own course separately from any contact with grace."[59]

Of course, there is also something right in an anticultural position that recognizes a necessity in "the movement of withdrawal and renunciation," as Niebuhr puts it.

> The relation of the authority of Jesus Christ to the authority of culture is such that every Christian must often feel himself claimed by the Lord to reject the world and its kingdoms [e.g., "the culture of death"] with their pluralism [e.g., "all religions are the same" or "right and wrong, truth and falsity, are relative to the individual"] and temporalism [this-worldliness], their makeshift compromises of many interests [resulting in the betrayal of orthodoxy], their hypnotic obsession by the love of [this] life [rather than the love of God] and the fear of death [rather than trusting in Christ's death and resurrection that defeated the power of death and frees us from the fear of our mortality].

Notwithstanding the necessity of this *ad hoc* strategy of withdrawal and renunciation, it must "be *followed by an equally necessary movement of responsible engagement in cultural tasks*," as Niebuhr correctly adds.[60] However, "withdrawal Christianity" is unable to make that move because it wrongly takes sanctification in Jesus Christ to mean renouncing creation as if creation itself were evil. Rejecting this withdrawal from the world as unbiblical, Dooyeweerd correctly remarks: "We have nothing to avoid in the world but *sin*. The war that the Christian wages

---

[59] Maritain, *On the Philosophy of History*, 130.
[60] Niebuhr, *Christ and Culture*, 68, italics added.

in God's power in this temporal life against the Kingdom of darkness, is a joyful struggle, not only for his own salvation, but for God's creation as a whole, which we do not hate, but love for Christ's sake. We must not hate anything in the world but *sin*."[61] Thus, making this movement of responsibly engaging in cultural tasks requires a theological affirmation of the world: "For everything created by God is good, and nothing is to be rejected if it is received with thanksgiving" (1 Tim. 4:4).

Christ *of* Culture

There is another typical answer, a highly influential one, which Christians—both Protestants and Catholics—have given to the question of how Christ is related to culture, and I know of no better word to describe its strategy than with the word *conformism*. The *leitmotif* of this strategy is accommodation, adaptation, updating, and inculturation of the Christian faith in order to *reconcile* it with some of the truth-claims, values, and basic orientation of modern secular culture. The assumption here is that the Church is somehow lagging behind modern cultural and intellectual developments and so it needs to catch up with them by updating its teaching. The result of this kind of adaptation is best called "cultural Protestantism" or "cultural Catholicism."[62] For cultural Christianity of either sort, however, the relationship between the Christian tradition and the modern secular consciousness is not one-sided. Rather, it is a two-sided relationship, a mutually critical correlation between faith and world, Christ and culture. As Niebuhr describes the two-sided relationship of cultural Christians:

> They feel no great tension between church and world,
> the social laws and the Gospel, the workings of divine
> grace and human effort, the ethics of salvation and

---

[61] Dooyeweerd, *A New Critique of Theoretical Thought*, 2:34.

[62] For a defense of "cultural Catholicism," see Dolan, *In Search of an American Catholicism*. For a similar defense, see also John T. McGreevy, *Catholicism and American Freedom: A History* (New York: W. W. Norton, 2003).

the ethics of social conservation or progress. *On the one hand* they interpret culture through Christ, regarding those elements in it as most important which are most accordant with his work and person; *on the other hand* they understood Christ through culture, selecting from his teaching and action as well as from the Christian doctrine about him such points as seem *to agree with what is best in civilization.* So they harmonize Christ and culture, not without excision, of course, from New Testament and social custom, of stubbornly discordant features. They do not necessarily seek Christian sanction for the whole of prevailing culture, but only for what they regard as real in the actual.[63]

Although I cannot argue fully the point here, I think there are three reasons why the accommodationist interpretation of inculturation is fundamentally flawed. *First,* regarding the question of how Christ should relate to culture, the cultural Christian is confronted by an answer of his own making in which Christianity increasingly loses its "transcendent" standpoint, that is, critical distance *over* culture because it seems to conceive of faith primarily as a religious experience of God without any determinate content, and as if beliefs were always generated only as a result of positive dialogue with the culture.[64] In other words, cultural Christianity seems to have abandoned the "dogmatical principle," as John Henry Newman called it, in which *revealed truth* about God, human beings, and the world is received, defended, and transmitted

---

[63] Niebuhr, *Christ and Culture*, 83–84 (italics added).

[64] Pushed to its extreme, this view leads to a cultural Catholicism that is radically pluralistic, indeed, relativistic. It is represented by contemporary lay Catholics who say, "'I'm afraid the church as a whole is coming to the point where it isn't one size fits all any more,' said Jack Scalione, 66, a turnpike inspector who was watching the papal funeral [of John Paul II] on television at Our Lady of Mount Carmel church in East Boston. 'What's good in Europe isn't necessarily good in America, and what's good in America isn't necessarily what's good in Latin America. You have to fit to the wishes of the people because the people are the church'" (*New York Times*, April 11, 2005, A16).

by Christians as something "definite, and formal, and independent of ourselves." This principle states that revealed truths have been "irrevocably committed to human language." This propositional revelation in verbalized form is at once *true* though *not exhaustive*,[65] "imperfect because it is human," adds Newman, "but definitive and necessary because given from above."[66] Furthermore, this classical view of revelation holds that revelation is at once God's self-revelation and the communication of divinely authorized truths. "And so," as Aidan Nichols correctly notes, "revelation has at one and the same time existential, cognitive, and ontological dimensions. In other words, it changes the human situation, our awareness of it, and our very being itself."[67]

My trouble with and hence resistance to the strategy of cultural Christianity does not stem from emphasizing the

---

[65] John Paul II, *Fides et Ratio*, 1998 Encyclical Letter,

> For faith clearly requires that human speech should in some universal way give expression—even though voiced analogically, but no less meaningfully—to divine, transcendent reality. Deprived of this assumption, the Word of God, which despite its use of human language remains divine, *could signify nothing of God*. The interpretation of this Word cannot merely keep tossing us from one interpretation to another, never directing us to a statement that is simple and true: were that the case there could be no revelation of God, but instead only the expression of human concepts about God and of the things it is presumed he thinks about us (no. 84; italics added).

The former Joseph Ratzinger, now Benedict XVI, remarks on John Paul II's very point: "Man is not caught in a hall of mirrors of interpretation; he can and must look for the way out to the reality that stands behind the words and manifests itself to him in and through the words" (*Truth and Tolerance: Christian Belief and World Religions*, trans. Henry Taylor [San Francisco: Ignatius Press, 2003], 189).

[66] John Henry Cardinal Newman, *An Essay on the Development of Christian Doctrine*, 6th ed. (1845; repr., Notre Dame: University of Notre Dame Press, 1989), chap. 7, sec. 5, par. 3, and sec. 1, par. 4, 348 and 325, respectively.

[67] Aidan Nichols, O.P. *Epiphany: A Theological Introduction to Catholicism* (Collegeville, Minn.: Liturgical Press, 1996), 32.

unchangeableness of our *understanding* of Christian truth and looking upon a restatement of Catholic teaching as a sign of apostasy. Not at all. Put positively, "The Church learned early in its history to express the Christian message in the concepts and language of different peoples and tried to clarify it in the light of the wisdom of their philosophies. It was an attempt to adapt the Gospel to the understanding of all men and the requirements of the learned, insofar as this could be done. Indeed, this kind of adaptation and preaching of the revealed Word must ever be the law of all evangelization."[68] Indeed, John XXIII's opening address at Vatican II points out that we can deepen our understanding of Catholic teaching by taking "a step forward toward a doctrinal penetration and a formation of [doctrinal] consciousness in faithful and perfect conformity to the authentic doctrine." The understanding of the faith can only be deepened without threatening its unchangeable truth if we hold to the following distinction made by John XXIII: "the deposit or the truths of faith, contained in our sacred teaching, are one thing, while the mode in which they are enunciated, keeping the same meaning and the same judgment, is another."[69] In other words, "the propositional truths of

---

[68] *Gaudium et Spes*, no. 44. When considered alone, without context, passages such as these have led some to misinterpret the meaning of inculturation as taught by the Second Vatican Council. Representative of such misinterpretations is that of Jay P. Dolan who suggests, as I understand him, that inculturation, in the sense of the Church's adapting and accommodating to the times, was John XXIII's major reason, if not the only reason, "for the council. He wanted to bring the church up to date, and to gain this goal he sought to establish a dialogue with people of other religions, with fellow Catholics, and with the world beyond the Church" (*In Search of An American Catholicism* [Oxford: Oxford University Press, 2002], 193). One of the major problems with this interpretation of inculturation is that it undervalues the critical and transformative dimensions of the Second Vatican Council's understanding of inculturation, as I will show in the text.

[69] Ioannes XXIII, "Allocutio habita d. 11 oct. 1962, in initio Concilii," 54 *Acta Apostolicae Sedis* (1962), 796, and for this quote, 792. This translation from the Latin of the opening address is from Germain Grisez, *The Way of the Lord Jesus*, 1:502.

faith are distinct from their linguistic expressions." The former are, if true, always and everywhere true; the latter may vary in our attempts to more clearly and accurately communicate revealed truths, but do not affect the truth of the propositions. Of course this understanding of the relationship between the truths of faith and their linguistic expression allows for doctrinal development. As Germain Grisez puts it,

> The fact is that truths of faith need nothing added to them to be true, but always need further truths of faith added to them to develop God's relationship to his people as he wishes it to develop.... [T]he Church always can bring such fresh truths from the riches of revelation. Since every such new truth is an aspect of the one truth revealed by God in the Lord Jesus, no authentic development of doctrine ever can contradict what the Church believed and taught in earlier times and other places.[70]

Second, the concept of inculturation is understood differently and, I think, more theologically correct, in the perspective of an "incarnational humanism," borrowing John Courtney Murray's phrase, where the "one overarching Christian endeavor [is]

---

[70] Grisez, *The Way of the Lord Jesus*, 1:496. See also, Vatican I, Dogmatic Constitution *Dei Filius* on the Catholic Faith (1870):

> For the doctrine of faith which God has revealed has not been proposed like a philosophical system to be perfected by human ingenuity, but has been committed to the spouse of Christ as divine trust to be faithfully kept and infallibly declared. Hence also that same meaning of the sacred dogmas is to be retained which our Holy Mother Church has once declared, and there must never be a deviation from that meaning on the specious ground and title of a more profound understanding. "Therefore, let there be growth and abundant progress in understanding, knowledge and wisdom, in each and all, in individuals and in the whole Church, at all times and in the succession of the ages, but only in its proper kind, i.e., in the same dogma, the same meaning, the same understanding" (c. 4).

the bringing of all things under the headship of Christ."[71] This perspective includes but goes beyond the emphasis of enjoining Christians to engage modern secular culture and enter into a positive dialogue with it. By contrast, the overarching endeavor of inculturation in the Christ *of* culture type is accommodation, updating, and adapting, which at best *undervalues*, or at worst *neglects*, the *transformationist* dynamic, or *conversionist* motif, of inculturation that is theologically rooted in the transcendent truth of the Incarnate Word, which is the objective self-revelation of the eternal Son of God, the second Person of the Holy Trinity, becoming man. As John Paul II explains, "Inculturation includes two dimensions: on the one hand, 'the intimate transformation of authentic cultural values through their integration in Christianity' and, on the other, 'the insertion of Christianity in the various human cultures.' The theological justification for inculturation is: "Just as 'the Word became flesh and dwelt among us' (John 1:14), so too the Good News, the Word of Jesus Christ proclaimed to the nations, *must take root* in the life-situation of the hearers of the Word. Inculturation is precisely this insertion of the Gospel message into cultures. For the Incarnation of the Son of God, precisely because it was complete and concrete, was also an incarnation in a particular culture. 'Every culture needs to be transformed by Gospel values in the light of the Paschal Mystery.'" Therefore, inculturation is both critical and transformative: "It is by looking at the Mystery of the Incarnation

---

[71] Murray, *We Hold These Truths*, 190. For a similar account linking inculturation to the lordship of Jesus Christ, see "Select Themes of Ecclesiology on the Occasion of the Eighth Anniversary of the Closing of the Second Vatican Council" in *International Theological Commission: Texts and Documents 1969–1985* (San Francisco, Ignatius, 1989), 267–316, and for the following quote, 281: "In the evangelization of cultures and the inculturation of the Gospel, a wondrous exchange is brought about: on the one hand, the Gospel reveals to each culture and sets free within it the final truth of the values which that culture carries. On the other hand, each and every culture expresses the Gospel in an original fashion and manifests new aspects of it. *This inculturation is an aspect of the recapitulation of all things in Christ* (Ephesians 1:10) and of the catholicity of the Church" (italics added).

and of the Redemption that the values and countervalues of cultures are to be discerned. Just as the Word of God became like us in everything but sin, so too the inculturation of the Good News takes on all authentic human values, purifying them from sin and restoring to them their full meaning."[72]

Third, the insurmountable dilemma that the cultural Christian now faces is one of his own making. As Niebuhr explains:

> In so far as part of its purposes is always that of recommending the gospel to an unbelieving society, or to some special group, such as the intelligentsia, or political liberals or conservatives, or workingmen, it often fails to achieve its end because *it does not go far enough, or because it is suspected of introducing an element that will weaken the cultural movement. It seems impossible to remove the offense of Christ and his cross even by means of these accommodations*; and cultural Christians share in the general limitation all Christianity encounters whether it fights or allies itself with the "world." *If the evangelists of the Christ of culture do not go far enough to meet the demands of men whose loyalty is primarily to the values of civilization, they go too far in the judgment of their fellow believers of other schools.* These point out that the cultural answers to the Christ-culture problem show a consistent tendency to distort the figure of the New Testament Jesus.[73]

---

[72] John Paul II, *Ecclesia in Africa*, 1995 Post-Synodal Apostolic Exhortation, nos. 59–61. See also the document prepared by the International Theological Commission, October 1988, "Faith and Inculturation," in *Catholicism and Secularization in America*, ed. David L. Schindler (Huntington, Ind.: Our Sunday Visitor, 1990), "Scandal for the Jews, the mystery of the Cross is foolishness to the pagans. Here the inculturation of the faith clashes with the radical sin of *idolatry* which keeps 'captive' the truth of a culture which is not assumed by Christ. As long as man is 'deprived of the glory of God' all that he 'cultivates' is nothing more than the opaque image of himself. The Pauline kerygma begins therefore with creation and the call to the covenant, denounces the moral perversions of blinded humanity, and announces salvation in the crucified and risen Christ" (224).

[73] Niebuhr, *Christ and Culture*, 108–9 (italics added).

Rather than making Christianity culturally relevant, this strategy *culturally marginalizes* Christianity precisely because in its accommodationist interpretation the cultural Christian offers the secular humanist "less and less in which to disbelieve."[74] Now, his fellow Christians will then protest not only that this is going too far in adapting Christianity to the times "where the faith so easily disappears into cultural dialogue"[75] but also, indeed chiefly, that this strategy has the opposite effect it set out to achieve, namely, it makes Christianity culturally irrelevant by no longer being distinctive enough to be needed in a dialogue. It is interesting to note here that it is often the critics of Christianity who wish that Christians would be more orthodox in their beliefs. Why do these critics insist upon this? They believe, rightly, I think, that there can be no serious dialogue with Christians beyond a certain point if they are not *integrally* Christian. As Jeffrey Stout once upon a time incisively put it, "One wants one's conversation partners to remain distinctive enough to be identified, to be needed."[76]

"Consequently," as Aidan Nichols rightly notes, "it is of the first importance to evangelization that the minds of the Church's members be not only alert to contemporary culture but also well-stocked with maturely reflected and apologetically honed dogmatic truth."[77]

---

[74] Alasdair MacIntyre, "The Fate of Theism," in *The Religious Significance of Atheism* (New York: Columbia University, 1969), 24. Similarly, Niebuhr says, "The cultural Christian … makes common cause with the nonbeliever to an extent which deprives him of distinctively Christian principles" (*Christ and Culture*, 143). Also helpful in understanding this dilemma was Van A. Harvey, "The Pathos of Liberal Theology," *Journal of Religion* 56 (1976): 382–91.

[75] Aidan Nichols, O.P., "Rerelating Faith and Culture," in *Christendom Awake: On Reenergizing the Church in Culture* (Grand Rapids: Eerdmans, 1999), 17.

[76] Jeffrey Stout, "The Voice of Theology in Contemporary Culture," in *Religion and America: Spirituality in a Secular Age*, ed. Mary Douglas and Steven M. Tipton (Boston: Beacon Press, 1983), 249–61, and for this quote, 260.

[77] Nichols, "Integral Evangelization," 70.

Christ *Fulfiller* of Culture

The third typical answer that Christians have given to the enduring question of how Christ relates to culture is, I believe, an advance on the second specifically where it affirms that culture is, unqualifiedly, neither good nor evil but rather is something that may be transformed and hence fulfilled through the critical and transformative truth of the Christian faith. Saint Thomas Aquinas' teaching that grace perfects nature, neither abolishing nor leaving it untouched, is a basic presupposition of this answer.[78]

What is the theological basis for claiming that culture is, unqualifiedly, neither good nor evil? Interestingly, neo-Calvinist Herman Dooyeweerd and John Paul II both take the gospel parable of the good grain and the weeds (cf. Matt. 13:24–30) growing together until the harvest as a "key to the entire history of mankind." This history, John Paul says, "is the 'theater' of the coexistence of good and evil" until the eschaton. "So even if evil exists alongside good," he adds, "good perseveres beside evil and grows, so to speak, from the same soil, namely human nature."[79] Significantly, both Dooyeweerd and John Paul affirm that God himself has imposed a definitive limit upon evil in light of the Redeemer, Jesus Christ. "The limit imposed upon evil by divine good has entered human history … through the work of Christ. So it is impossible to separate Christ from human history." That is, "it is impossible to think of the limit placed by God himself upon … evil without reference to the mystery of Redemption." This is so only for this reason, says John Paul: "The Paschal Mystery

---

[78] On this, see St. Thomas Aquinas, *Summa Theologiae*, I, q. 1, art. 8, resp. 2, "Grace does not abolish nature, but perfects it." See also, *De veritate*, q. 14, art. 10, ad 9. For a brief discussion of Aquinas on nature and grace, see W. D. Hughes, O.P., "The Infusion of Virtues," Appendix 3, in St. Thomas Aquinas, *Summa Theologiae*, vol. 23, *Virtue* (New York: McGraw-Hill, 1975), 247–48.

[79] John Paul II, *Memory and Identity*, 4. See also, Herman Dooyeweerd, *A New Critique of Theoretical Thought*, 1:523.

confirms that good is ultimately victorious, that life conquers death and that love triumphs over hate."[80]

Now, Dooyweerd takes the idea that Christ limits evil, given that "the antithesis between sin and creation is *really* abrogated by his redemptive work," and develops it by being more specific than John Paul II regarding the sense in which Christ limits, checks, or restrains the operation and power of sin. He does so by appealing to Abraham Kuyper's notion of common grace.[81] Kuyper distinguishes between common grace and particular (or special) grace: The former is a "temporal restraining grace, which holds back and blocks the effect of sin"; the latter is a "saving grace, which in the end abolishes sin and completely undoes its consequences."[82] These two forms of grace, special and common, have a common origin in Christ, which Kuyper explains as follows.

> If we consult Scripture we will find it clearly spelled out that the ... self-same Christ is simultaneously two things: the root of the life of creation as well as the root of the life of the new creation. First we read that Christ is "the first-born of all creation, for in him all things

---

[80] John Paul II, *Memory and Identity*, 15, 19, 21, and for this quote, 55.

[81] Abraham Kuyper gives the first constructive theological analysis of the Reformed doctrine of common grace in his three volume work, *De Gemeene Gratie* ["Common Grace"]—published 1902, 1903, and 1904, respectively by Höveker & Wormser in Amsterdam. For a selection from these volumes, see "Common Grace," in *Abraham Kuyper: A Centennial Reader*, ed. James D. Bratt, 165–201 (Grand Rapids: Eerdmans, 1998). On the development of Kuyper's mature views regarding the relationship between common grace and Christ's redemption, see the magisterial study of S. U. Zuidema, "Common Grace and Christian Action in Abraham Kuyper," in *Communication and Confrontation: A Philosophical Appraisal and Critique of Modern Society and Contemporary Thought* (Toronto: Wedge, 1972), 52–104. For a contemporary discussion of the doctrine of common grace, see Richard J. Mouw, *He Shines in All That's Fair: Culture and Common Grace*, Stob Lectures (Grand Rapids: Eerdmans, 2001). For a general introduction to Kuyper's thought, see Peter S. Heslam, *Creating a Christian Worldview: Abraham Kuyper's Lectures on Calvinism* (Grand Rapids: Eerdmans, 1998).

[82] Kuyper, *Abraham Kuyper: A Centennial Reader*, 168 (*De Gemeene Gratie*, 1:222).

were created, in heaven and on earth," so that he is "before all things and in him all things hold together" [Col. 1:15–17]. It could hardly be stated more plainly and clearly that Christ is the root of the creation and therefore of common grace, for it is common grace that prevents things from sinking into nothingness. (Does not the text say that all things *hold together* in him?) But we immediately note in the second place that the same Christ is "the *Head of the Body* and the first-born from the dead" [Colossians 1:18], hence also the root of the life of the new creation or special grace. The two things are even stated in parallel terms: he is the root of common grace for he is *the first born of all creation* [v. 15], and simultaneously the root of special grace, for he the *first-born from the dead* [v. 18]. There is thus no doubt whatever that common grace and special grace come most intimately connected from their origin, and this connection lies in Christ.[83]

Yet, there is one more point I need to make about the relationship between common grace and particular grace in order

---

[83] Kuyper, *Abraham Kuyper: A Centennial Reader*, 186–87 (*De Gemeene Gratie*, 2:645; see also 183). I am reminded here of John Paul II who in his 1998 Encyclical Letter, *Fides et Ratio*, makes a similar point about the selfsame Christ.

The unity of truth is a fundamental premise of human reasoning, as the principle of non-contradiction makes clear. Revelation renders this unity certain, showing that the God of creation is also the God of salvation history. It is the one and the same God who establishes and guarantees the intelligibility and reasonableness of the natural order of things … and who reveals himself as the Father of our Lord Jesus Christ. This unity of truth, natural and revealed, is embodied in a living and personal way in Christ, as the Apostle [Paul] reminds us: "Truth is in Jesus" (cf. Eph 4:21; Col 1:15–20). He is the *eternal Word* in whom all things were created, and he is the *incarnate Word* who in his entire person reveals the Father (cf. John 1:14, 18).… [W]hat is revealed in him is 'the full truth' (cf. John 1:14–16) of everything which was created in him and through him and which therefore in him finds its fulfillment (cf. Col 1:17). (no. 34)

to avoid the image that they run along parallel tracks, existing independently side-by-side, with completely independent purposes, having only an extrinsic relationship to each other. The purpose of common grace does not exist outside of particular grace, given that the latter "restores creation in its root." In other words, Kuyper rightly sees that nature and grace belong together. "You cannot see grace in all its riches if you do not perceive how its tiny roots and fibers everywhere penetrate into the joints and cracks of the life of nature. And you cannot validate that connectedness [between nature and grace] if, with respect to grace, you first look at the salvation of your soul and primarily on the *Christ of God*." Kuyper explains:

> For if grace exclusively concerned atonement for sin and salvation of souls, one could view grace as something located and operating outside of nature. One could picture it as oil poured on turbulent waters, floating on those waters while remaining *separate* from them, solely so that the drowning person can save his life by grabbing the life buoy thrown out to him. But if it is true that Christ our Savior has to do not only with our soul but also with our body, that all things in the world belong to Christ and are claimed by him, that one day he will triumph over every enemy in that world, and that in the end Christ will not gather a few separated souls around him, as is the case now, but will rule as king on a new earth under a new heaven—then, of course, everything is different.
>
> For that reason Scripture continually points out that the *Savior* of the world is also the *Creator* of the world, indeed that he could become its Savior only *because* he already was its *Creator*. Of course, it was not the *Son of man*, not the *incarnate Word*, who created the world.... Still, Scripture repeatedly points out that he, the first-born of the dead, is also the first-born of creation, that the Word Incarnate nevertheless always was and remained the same eternal Word who was with God and was God, of whom it is written that without that Word nothing was made that is made [John 1:1–3].

> Christ then is connected with *nature* because he is its Creator, and at the same time connected to *grace* because, as Re-creator, he manifested the riches of grace in the midst of that nature.[84]

Turning now back to Dooyeweerd after this brief introduction to Kuyper's doctrine of common grace, we can understand the specific sense in which Christ limits evil. Says Dooyeweerd,

> Common grace in the first place consists in the maintenance of the temporal world-order in all its structures against the disintegration by sin. In this sense common grace embraces "the evil and the good together" and is restricted to temporal life. Special grace, however, is concerned with the renewal of the religious root of the creation in Christ Jesus as the Head of the regenerated human race and [hence] must not [be] considered in an *individualistic* soteriological sense. From this it follows that particular grace is the real root and foundation of common grace. It is therefore absolutely contrary to the Biblical standpoint when a distinction is made between two independent realms or spheres of grace.[85]

He explains, following Kuyper, that Christ's redemption is the source of common grace, in other words, the source of a restraining or "preserving grace," which is "a counterforce against the destructive work of sin in the cosmos."

> Common grace is meaningless without Christ as the root and head of the regenerated human race.... It is grace shown to mankind as a whole, which is regenerate in its new root Jesus Christ, but has not yet been loosened from its old apostate root. This is the meaning of Jesus' parable of the tares among the wheat. The wheat and the tares must grow together until the harvest.... It is all due to God's common grace in Christ that there are still means left in the temporal world to resist the

---

[84] Kuyper, *Abraham Kuyper: A Centennial Reader*, 173 (*De Gemeene Gratie*, 1:228).

[85] Dooyeweerd, *A New Critique of Theoretical Thought*, 3:506–7.

> destructive force of the elements that have got loose;
> that there are still means to combat disease, to check
> psychic maladies, to practice logical thinking, to save
> cultural development from going down into savage bar-
> barism, to develop language, to preserve the possibility
> of social intercourse, to withstand injustice, and so on.
> All these things are the fruits of Christ's work
>   … From the very beginning God has viewed His
> fallen creation in the light of the Redeemer.[86]

Thus, we are now in a position to understand why it is when we survey cultures from a Christian standpoint, we see *both* goodness *and* fallenness, grace *and* sin, *both* truth *and* falsity. It follows from this point that the Christian should accept truth and goodness wherever it appears among fallen human beings, even among unbelievers. Of course the grasp of truth in that context may be incomplete, inadequate, even distorted, but because the Spirit of God is the sole foundation of all that is true, we honor him by accepting that truth. *All truth is God's truth*.[87]

This is by no means the whole picture. "The good news of Christ continually renews the life and culture of fallen man; it combats and removes the error and evil which flow from the ever-present attraction of sin. It never ceases to purify and

---

[86] Dooyeweerd, *A New Critique of Theoretical Thought*, 1:523, and 2:34–35.

[87] Both St. Thomas Aquinas (1225–1274) and, centuries later, the Protestant reformer John Calvin (1509–1564) held similar views on this score. Aquinas wrote, "Although some minds are enwrapped in darkness, that is, deprived of clear and meaningful knowledge, yet there is no human mind in such darkness as not to participate in some of the divine light … because all that is true by whomsoever it is uttered, comes from the Holy Spirit." I found this passage by Aquinas in John Paul II, "Method and Doctrine of St. Thomas in Dialogue with Modern Culture," in *The Whole Truth about Man*, ed. with an intro. by James V. Schall, S.J. (Boston: Daughters of St. Paul, 1981), 268–69. Similarly, Calvin wrote: "If we regard the Spirit of God as the sole fountain of truth, we shall neither reject the truth itself, nor despise it wherever it shall appear, unless we wish to dishonor the Spirit of God" (*Institutes of the Christian Religion*, ed. John T. McNeill [Philadelphia: Westminster, 1960], 2.2.15.273–74).

elevate the morality of peoples. It takes the spiritual qualities and endowments of every age and nation, and with supernatural riches it causes [man's life and culture] to blossom, as it were, from within; it fortifies, completes and restores them in Christ" (*GS*, no. 58).

At this point I move on to unpack the claim that Christ is the fulfiller of culture by attempting to give a definition of culture in order to get a better grasp of what exactly is being fulfilled. We may define a culture, following Charles Taylor, as a specific intellectual, moral, symbolic, and institutional formation manifesting an embodied understanding of "personhood, social relations, states of mind/soul, goods and bads, virtues and vices" or "a constellation of understandings of person, nature, society, and the good" as well as about the relationships of the human person to "God, the cosmos and other humans."[88] Man is a culture-bearing creature whose cultures are diverse; permeable, which includes an openness to influence from each other; and changeable because he is developing and therefore historical.[89]

In particular, says the former Joseph Cardinal Ratzinger, now Benedict XVI, "Each particular culture not only lives out its own experience of God, the world, and man, but on its path it necessarily encounters other cultural agencies and has to react to their quite different experiences." In that intercultural exchange, he adds, "that culture's own perceptions and values [may be] deepened and purified," leading to a "profound reshaping of that culture's previous form" (*TT*, 63). Yet, this is precisely where the objection is raised that this exchange

---

[88] Charles Taylor, "Two Theories of Modernity," *Hastings Center Report*, 25, no. 2 (March-April 1995): 24–33, and for these quotes 24, 29. I discovered this reference to Taylor in Tracey Rowland, *Culture and the Thomist Tradition After Vatican II* (New York: Routledge, 2003), 12–13. Similar definitions of culture can be found in Niebuhr, *Christ and Culture*, 32–39. See also, Ratzinger, *Truth and Tolerance*, 60–63. Subsequent references to *TT* will be made parenthetically in the text.

[89] Nichols, "Rerelating Faith and Culture," 10–11.

is necessarily violent of that culture and alienating it from its own specific cultural formation. If so, then even inculturating the gospel and evangelizing in the faith-knowledge of the great and universal commission that Jesus Christ himself gave his disciples is unjustified (Matt. 28:19f.). Behind this objection is the assumption that there is no universal truth about God, man, or reality, which is in principle accessible to all men and belongs to all. We are left with the idea that we are only, in differing cultural formations, as Benedict puts it, "just touching on the mystery that never unveils itself to us" (*TT*, 57). "Thus the multiplicity of cultures serves to demonstrate the relativism of all cultures. *Culture is set against truth.* This relativism, which is nowadays to be found, as a basic attitude of enlightened people, penetrating far into the realm of theology, is the most profound difficulty of our age" (*TT*, 72; italics added).

Benedict XVI faces this difficulty head on. "Only if it is true that all cultures are potentially universal and have an inner capacity to be open to others can interculturality lead to new and fruitful forms [of culture]" (*TT*, 64). He undercuts the assumption of relativism by arguing that inculturation "assumes the potential universality of every culture" (*TT*, 59). That is, the union of all cultures is in principle possible because the "same human nature is at work in all of them and there is a common truth of humanity alive within that human nature that aims towards union" (*TT*, 60). There is more: the very same Logos who has become man in Jesus Christ, the self-revelation of truth itself, is at work in all these various cultural formations leading them toward truth. If this is so, then no violence is necessarily being done to a specific cultural formation because each and every culture is *commonly oriented*, in light of our common human nature, *to the truth of our humanity*. "A meeting of cultures is possible because man, in all the variety of his history and of his social structures and customs, is *a single being, one and the same. This one being, man, is however touched and affected in the very depth of his existence by truth itself*"

(*TT*, 64–65; italics added). This common truth of humanity is that man is *created by God and for God*, that God unceasingly draws man to himself, and that only in communion with God will he find the truth and wholeness for which he never stops searching (cf. *CCC*, nos. 27–30). Thus, inculturating the faith as well as evangelizing others "opens up" and further develops the direction of a specific cultural formation to the common truth of humanity. The truth to be found in a given formation coexists with falsehood. If I understand Benedict XVI correctly, then, a critical engagement with those cultures is required, not merely to discern falsehoods, but also to "open up" the fragments of truth found there in the direction of Christ, with the aim of assimilating that truth into a larger synthesis, "within which the truth about God and about reality as a whole is always involved" (*TT*, 66). "A process of this kind can in fact lead to a breaking open of the silent alienation of man from the truth and from himself that exists within that culture … to let itself be purified and thus to become better adapted to the truth and to man" (*TT*, 63, 60). Because of the potential universality of every culture, breaking open their fragments of truth in the direction of Christ will lead to a full unfolding of the truth.[90]

Because no culture is unqualifiedly either good or evil, then "whatever elements in any culture exclude such opening up … represent what is inadequate in that culture" (*TT*, 60). In some cases, however, intercultural exchange may lead to the recognition of the limits of some specific cultural outlook or formation and hence to *complementary* perspectives that are neither contradictory nor self-sufficient but rather "incomplete and

---

[90] John Paul II, *Fides et Ratio*, no. 71. See also, "Faith and Inculturation," 220: "One conviction dominates the preaching of Jesus: in Jesus—in his word and in his person—God perfects the gifts he has already made to Israel and to all nations, by transcending them. *Jesus is the sovereign light and true wisdom for all nations and all cultures*" (italics added).

approximate portrayals of an enormously complex reality."[91] Therefore, says Benedict, "only in the interrelating of all great works of culture can man approach the unity and wholeness of his true nature" (*TT*, 65). Next, intercultural exchange may also lead to the recognition that different cultural formations are *genetically* related as "successive stages in some process of development. Each later stage presupposes earlier stages, partly to include them, and partly to transform them."[92] Most importantly, however, the perspectives embedded in cultural formations may also be "opposed *dialectically*." "What for one is true, for another is false. What for one is good, for another is evil."[93] Indeed, says Benedict, "the potential universality of cultures is often blocked by quite insurmountable obstacles that prevent it from turning into an actual universality." Thus: "Not only a [common] dynamic exists, but equally [common] divisions, barriers against others, contradictions that exclude, an impossibility of transition because the waters between are far too deep. This [is] a negative factor in human existence: an alienation that hinders our perceiving things and that, *at least partially*, cuts men off from the truth and thus also from each other" (*TT*, 65; italics added). Notwithstanding these negative dynamics, the openness to the truth endures within human nature and hence "every culture contains within itself and displays an indestructible urge for some sort of fulfillment." "We can therefore say," adds John Paul II, "that culture contains within itself the capacity for receiving divine revelation," which is "the immutable truth of God, which he himself has revealed in the history and culture of a people."[94]

---

[91] Bernard Lonergan, S.J., *Method in Theology* (New York: Herder and Herder, 1972), 219.

[92] Lonergan, *Method in Theology*, 236.

[93] Lonergan, *Method in Theology*, 236.

[94] John Paul II, *Fides et Ratio*, no. 71.

At this point, what is special about the self-understanding of Christian faith can be seen. It knows very well, if it is aware and uncorrupted, that there is a great deal of what is human in its particular cultural forms, *a great deal that needs purifying and opening up*. But it is also certain that it is at heart the self-revelation of truth itself [the Logos who has become man, Jesus Christ] and, therefore, redemption. For the real problem of mankind is the darkening of truth. This distorts our action and sets us against one another, because we bear our own evil within ourselves, are alienated from ourselves, cut off from the ground of our being, from God. If truth is offered, this means a leading out of alienation and thus out of the state of division; it means the vision of a common standard that does no violence to any culture but that guides each one to its own heart, because each exists ultimately as an expectation of truth.... It is then clear that this truth is the sphere within which everyone can find and relate to one another and, in so doing, lose nothing of his own value or his own dignity. (*TT*, 65–67, 72)

Thus, on the one hand, the Christian faith is open to all that is true, good, and beautiful in world cultures. Significantly, it will also oppose "whatever in the culture bars the doors against the gospel." "Therefore," adds Benedict, "it has always been critical of culture also, and it must continue fearlessly and steadfastly to critique culture, especially today."[95] The assumption here is that whatever good is found sown in, say, Greek thought, in the minds and hearts of men such as Plato, Aristotle, Plotinus, and others, must be taken captive for the truth of Christ and for the glory of God (cf. 2 Cor. 10:5). In short, in Etienne Gilson's wonderfully apt phrase, Christian thinkers must "put these fragments of truth in the service of

---

[95] Pope Benedict XVI, "Communication and Culture," in *On the Way to Jesus Christ*, trans. Michael J. Miller (San Francisco: Ignatius Press, 2005), 42–52, and for this quote, 49.

revelation."[96] This service is, as Hans Urs von Balthasar rightly urges, "no mechanical adoption of alien chains of thought with which one can adorn and garland the Christian dimension externally."[97] In other words, as Calvin Seerveld puts it, "The re-forming Christian approach to unchristian culture is not one of highway robbery and synthetic adoption but is one of serious, anti-sympathetic vibration, if you can take a metaphor; in forming, in building a re-formational Christian culture we scrutinize unchristian genius (to know what is going on!) to see what they are mistakenly getting at in God's world and to use them for a good thing in fashioning our own wineskins."[98] Thus, the task implied in Gilson's phrase could be distinguished, says Balthasar, into the "art of *breaking open* all finite, philosophical truth in the direction of Christ, and the art of

---

[96] Etienne Gilson, *The Philosopher and Theology*, trans. Ralph MacDonald, C.S.B., (London: Sheed & Ward, 1939). 188. Gilson's approach stands in the line of the "spoils from Egypt" trope. For an important discussion of this trope, see Fr. Thomas G. Guarino, *Foundations of Systematic Theology* (New York: T&T Clark, 2005), 269–310. He explains this trope as one "that characterized the work of so many early Christian writers. Insofar as God had created the world, had communicated himself to humanity by a primordial act of grace and love inscribed in creation itself, wisdom and truth could be found in many places. All such wisdom, however, the traditional spoils metaphor insists, must ultimately be disciplined by, and incorporated into, the revelatory narrative. Athens, whatever its own insights into truth, must ultimately be chastened by Jerusalem" (269).

[97] Hans Urs von Balthasar, "On the Tasks of Catholic Philosophy in Our Time," *Communio: International Catholic Review* 20 (Spring 1993): 147–87, and for this quote, 155–56. That Balthasar's point is in agreement with Aquinas may be seen from the following statement of Aquinas: "So those who use the works of the philosophers in sacred doctrine, by bringing them into the service of faith, do not mix water with wine, but rather change water into wine" (Questions 1–4 of Aquinas' *Commentary on the* De Trinitate *of Boethius*, trans. with intro. and notes Armand Maurer [Toronto: Pontifical Institute of Medieval Studies, 1987], Q. 2, art. 3, reply 5.) Clearly, Aquinas also rejects, in Balthasar's words, a "mechanical adoption of alien chains of thought with which one can adorn and garland the Christian dimension externally."

[98] Calvin Seerveld, *A Christian Critique of Art and Literature* (Ontario: Association for Reformed Scientific Studies, 1964), 27.

clarifying transposition."[99] Regarding the former, Christians are deeply committed to the "all-embracing authority of Christ" (cf. Matt. 28:18) over all forms of creaturely truth because in Christ are hid all the treasures of wisdom and knowledge (cf. Col. 2:2–3), and hence Christians "cannot rest until they have brought all these forms of truth into the service of the one truth. 'Everything is yours; but you belong to Christ, and Christ to God' (1 Cor. 3:23).'"[100] Regarding the art of clarifying transposition, Balthasar writes,

> The fragment or stone that they pick up may come from the bed of a Christian stream, or of a pagan or heretical stream, but they know how to cleanse it and to polish it until that radiance shines forth which shows that it is a fragment of the total glorification of God. Such a methodology may appear dangerous, because the clear and sharp outlines of the evangelical decision threaten to become blurred in it. This is the form of thought which necessarily *had* to be confused by unbelieving criticism with the syncretism of late Antiquity, the form of thought which permitted Christianity to amalgamate itself with the elements of Hellenism which were alien to its own being. But everything depends here on the disposition in which the synthesis is made: if the knowledge of the absoluteness of the truth of Christ stands at the abiding origin of such thought, and if the decision for him has been made with the entire purity of a loving soul, then it is legitimate and safe to adopt the intellectual mission to go out into all the world and to take captive all truth for Christ. "Test *everything* and retain what is good!" (1 Thess. 5:21). But "do not conform yourselves to the spirit of the world" (Rom. 12:2).[101]

---

[99] Balthasar, "On the Tasks of Catholic Philosophy in Our Time," 156.
[100] Balthasar, "On the Tasks of Catholic Philosophy in Our Time," 158.
[101] Balthasar, "On the Tasks of Catholic Philosophy in Our Time," 159.

Benedict illustrates this "path of cultural encounter and con-flict" by using an image from the writings of the fourth-century Cappadocian, Basil of Caesarea (ca. 330–379), who took the same path with the Greek culture of his time. "I was one who slits the fruit of the sycamore" (Amos 7:14). Basil writes:

> The sycamore is a tree that bears very plentiful fruit. But it is tasteless unless one carefully slits it and allows its saps to run out, whereby it becomes flavorful. That is why, we believe, the sycamore is a symbol for the pagan world; it offers a surplus, yet at the same it is insipid. This comes from living according to pagan customs. When one manages to slit them by means of the Logos, it [the pagan world] is transformed, becomes tasty and useful.[102]

Benedict cites a recent German commentator of Basil's passage that is illuminating:

> In this symbol [of the sycamore] are found the plente-ousness, the wealth, the luxuriance of the pagan world …, but its deficiency is found therein as well. As it is, it is insipid, unusable. It needs a complete transfor-mation, whereby the change does not destroy its sub-stance; rather, it gives to it the qualities it lacks.… The fruit remains fruit; its abundance is not diminished; rather it is recognized as an advantage.… On the other hand, the necessary transformation can scarcely be more keenly evident in this image than through the fact that what formerly could not be enjoyed now becomes edible. In the "running out" of the sap, furthermore, the process of purification is suggested.[103]

One final point, adds Benedict XVI, is that the source of the transformation alluded to above is not internal to the tree itself and its fruit. In keeping with the image of the shepherd and the dresser of the sycamore tree, an intervention from

---

[102] Benedict XVI, "Communication and Culture," 46.
[103] Benedict XVI, "Communication and Culture," 47.

outside is necessary. Says Benedict, "Applied to the pagan world, to what is characteristic of human culture, this means: The Logos itself must slit our cultures and their fruit, so that what is unusable is purified and becomes not only usable but good...." Yes, ultimately only the Logos himself can guide our cultures to their true purity and maturity, but the Logos makes us his servants, the "dresser of sycamore trees.... An ongoing and patient encounter between the Logos and the culture is necessary, mediated by the service of the faithful."[104]

I do not think it is reaching too far to suggest that the "dresser of the sycamore trees" resonates with the words of Jesus to his disciples recorded in the gospel of Matthew, "The harvest is plentiful but the workers are few. Ask the Lord of the harvest, therefore, to send out workers into His harvest field" (9:37–38). Indeed, deeply mindful of the words of Saint Paul, "I am not ashamed of the Gospel: it is the power of God for salvation to every one who has faith" (Rom. 1:16), the Christian cannot help but proclaim the gospel in the conviction that Jesus Christ is the answer to the question that is every human life. Jesus Christ, the revelation of truth itself, is the Way, the Truth, and the Life (cf. John 14:6). "In reality it is only in the mystery of the Word made flesh that the mystery of man truly becomes clear" (GS, no. 22). Christ alone, not only reconciles us to the Father but also reveals the totality of the mystery of man. "He is the truth in person and, thereby, the way to be human" (TT, 67). That is the "high claim" (TT, 67) to truth that the Christian faith brings, indeed *must* bring, to the cultures of the world.

Christ *and* Culture

Some versions of the fourth approach—typically called *dualism*—to the enduring question of how Christ relates to culture urge us to distinguish the progress *of* history from the

---

[104] Benedict XVI, "Communication and Culture," 47.

progressive realization of the kingdom of God *within* history because the final consummation of all things is an eschatological event. The kingdom of God is both present and future, both now and not yet. In and by the singularly unique revelation of Jesus Christ, the kingdom of God is presently inaugurated but it will reach its final consummation only when the Lord Jesus returns to bring about the renewal of all things: "Behold, I make all things new" (Rev. 21:5). For the present, between the already and the not yet, all our works, including the works of culture, the structures of society, are fallen and distorted by sin. The reason then for insisting on distinguishing the progress *of* history from the progress of the kingdom of God *within* history is clear: "*Before the holiness of God* as disclosed in the grace of Jesus Christ ... there is corruption and degradation in all man's work." There exists a tension between faith and culture that manifests a *dualism* between sin and grace, that is, "the situation of cultured, sinful man confronting the holiness of divine grace." Short of eschatological fulfillment, then, Christ's lordship and historical progress is not one and the same thing. John Paul II puts this point admirably well:

> Man, who was created for freedom, bears within himself the wound of original sin, which constantly draws him towards evil and puts him in need of redemption. Not only is *this doctrine an integral part of Christian revelation*; it also has great hermeneutical value insofar as it helps one to understand human reality. Man tends towards good, but he [is] also capable of evil.... [Thus] when people think they possess the secret of a perfect social organization which makes evil impossible, they also think that they can use any means, including violence and deceit, in order to bring that organization into being. Politics then becomes a 'secular religion' which operates under the illusion of creating paradise in this world. But no political society—which possesses its own autonomy and laws—can ever be confused with the Kingdom of God. The Gospel parable of the weeds among the wheat (cf. Matt. 13:24–30, 36–43)

teaches that it is for God alone to separate the subjects of the Kingdom from the subjects of the Evil One, and that this judgment will take place at the end of time. By presuming to anticipate judgment here and now, man puts himself in the place of God and sets himself against the patience of God.[105]

This version of dualism is, therefore, a needed *corrective* to the optimism that is implied by views that identify the growth of the kingdom of God with human progress. In this respect, dualism, or at least some versions of it, shares with anticultural Christianity a profound sense of sin even in the whole world of human activity. Unlike the latter, however, "the dualist knows that he belongs to that culture and cannot get out of it, that God indeed sustains him in it and by it; for if God in His grace did not sustain the world in its sin it would not exist for a moment."[106] Notwithstanding this positive note, this view raises the important question of whether it leaves cultural life and its institutions with a merely *negative* function in a fallen world—restraining sin from becoming as destructive as it might otherwise be—rather than with a certain *positive* value of its own.[107] It leaves unanswered the equally important question of whether living the Christian life here and now in the temporal world is necessary because intrinsically meaningful for the realization of God's redemptive work.[108]

Significantly, humanism in the last several centuries has reacted against this version of dualism by asserting "the autonomy and inherent worth of human life in this world."[109] Obviously, the orthodox Christian faith rejects the notion of autonomy and inherent worth when that is understood as a self-sufficiency entailing a denial, as it surely does for many,

---

[105] John Paul II, *Centesimus Annus*, no. 25.

[106] Niebuhr, *Christ and Culture*, 152–53, 156.

[107] Niebuhr, *Christ and Culture*, 171.

[108] Again, helpful here with the formulation of this question is Germain Grisez, *The Way of the Lord Jesus*, 1:16–17, 1:807–30.

[109] Grisez, *The Way of the Lord Jesus*, 1:811.

of the theology of creation—"every creature, man included, naturally depends upon God"[110]—and the theology of the Incarnation: "The Truth is that only in the mystery of the Incarnate Word does the mystery of man take on light" (*GS*, no. 22; cf. no. 36). Unfortunately, however, some Christians—both Protestant and Catholic—have framed their whole concept of the Christian life with the understanding that nature and grace are separated into two quasi-independent orders of reality, namely, one temporal, the other spiritual, one natural, and the other supernatural. This "parallelistic dualism of separated spiritual and temporal life," as Niebuhr describes this concept,[111] entails the idea of the autonomy of the temporal order, meaning thereby that this order falls outside the scope of the fall into sin as well as being unrelated to, or autonomous from, grace.

This concept leads Christians to *live double rather than integral lives*, putting their faith and their daily lives into separate compartments, which the Second Vatican Council called one of the most serious errors of our age (cf. *GS*, no. 43). Most importantly, this dualistic concept of nature and grace leaves nature untouched by grace. It has not been radically affected by sin and therefore is not in need of renewal and transformation in its own realm. This results in a cultural naturalism or secularism. Unlike anticultural Christians who take nature to be so corrupt that grace, no longer able to transform it, merely replaces it altogether by adding the spiritual realm over and above creation, this dualistic concept leaves nature untouched by grace and, in the process, effectively limits the scope of sin and redemption to the supernatural realm.[112] In

---

[110] John Paul II, *Fides et Ratio*, no. 80.

[111] Niebuhr, *Christ and Culture*, 179.

[112] Especially influential in my thinking on the relationship between nature and grace have been the reflections of Dutch neo-Calvinist philosopher Dooyeweerd (1894–977). For a brief introduction to his thinking, see *In the Twilight of Western Thought*. Extremely helpful also to me was De Lubac, *The Mystery of the Supernatural*. See also, David L. Schindler, "Introduction: Grace and the Form of Nature and Culture," 10–30, esp. 11, 20–21.

other words, *cultural life, indeed the whole of temporal life, does not need Christ!*

In the early twentieth century, the great French Catholic thinker, Jacques Maritain wisely noted that it is erroneous to ignore both the distinction between nature and grace as well as their union.[113] There remains to ask how best to understand the union of nature and grace. The brief answer to this question here must be that *grace restores nature*, meaning thereby the totality of created reality. In the words of Henri Cardinal De Lubac, "The supernatural does not merely *elevate* (this traditional term is correct, but it is inadequate by itself) ... [Rather] it *transforms it* ... 'Behold, I make all things new!' (Rev. 21:5). Christianity is 'a doctrine of transformation' because the Spirit of Christ comes to permeate the first creation and make of it a 'new creature.' What is true of the final great transformation, on the occasion of the 'Parousia' at which there will arise 'new heavens and a new earth' (Rev. 21), is already true now, according to Saint Paul, of each one of us."[114]

Christ *Saving Transformer* of Culture

Shortly before his death, the Holy Father, John Paul II, published his final book, thus leaving the Church, indeed the whole of humanity, the beautiful gift of his reflections entitled, *Memory and Identity*. Relevant to the question of the indivisible unity of nature and grace is the following passages from this work:

> The resurrection of Christ clearly illustrated that only the measure of good introduced by God into history through the mystery of Redemption is sufficient to correspond fully to the truth of the human being. The

---

[113] Maritain, *Clairvoyance de Rome*, 222 (italics added), "*There is one error that consists in ignoring the distinction between nature and grace. There is another that consists in ignoring their union.*" I discovered this quote in De Lubac, "Apologetics and Theology," 91–104, and this citation at 103n28.

[114] De Lubac, *A Brief Catechesis on Nature and Grace*, 81–82.

> Paschal Mystery thus becomes the definitive measure of man's existence in the world created by God. In this mystery, not only is eschatological truth revealed to us, that is to say the fullness of the Gospel, or Good News. There also shines forth a light to enlighten the whole of human existence in its temporal dimension and this light is then reflected onto the created world. Christ, through his Resurrection, has so to speak "justified" the work of creation, and especially the creation of man. He has "justified" it in the sense that he revealed the 'just measure" of good intended by God at the beginning of human existence. This measure is not merely what was provided by him in creation and then compromised by man through sin; it is a superabundant measure, in which the original plan finds a higher realization (cf. Gen. 3:14–15). In Christ, man is called to a new life, as son in the Son, the perfect expression of God's glory.[115]

At the core of the Christian worldview is an interlocking set of life-orienting beliefs regarding the creation, fall into sin, and Redemption (i.e., incarnation, passion, resurrection, and ascension). First, God created the world good. Given the cultural mandate to subdue and have dominion over created reality, this "goodness" extends to the work of man's hands when accomplished in the light of "the truth about ourselves and about the world."[116] Indeed, the totality of creation, especially man who is its crown, actually manifests God's goodness, being created in the image and likeness of God. This manifestation of goodness is God's thesis, his affirmation, his *yes* to the creation (Gen. 1:31).

Second, all creation (i.e., nature, culture, history, society) is fallen through original sin. Human nature as a whole has lost its original harmony, and man is wounded at the very root of his being, estranged from God, from himself, and from

---

[115] John Paul II, *Memory and Identity*, 25.
[116] John Paul II, *Memory and Identity*, 81.

his fellow man. His humanity exhibits the marks of being sinful, prone to sin, with sin being a violation of God's will and purpose. This sinfulness denies God's thesis and has its beginnings in Genesis 3. God's response to man's sin is *yes* but also *no*. *Yes*, because God, full of love, mercy, and grace does not abandon the fallen creation. Indeed, Genesis 3:15 contains the first proclamation of the Messiah, the *proto-evangelium*; also *no*, because God, judging man in the light of his perfect justice and holiness is the author of the antithesis, of the sign of contradiction between good and evil; between the seed of the woman and the seed of the serpent.

Third, the redemption accomplished through the mystery of the Incarnation and Christ's finished work—his life, passion, death, resurrection, and ascension—abrogates the antithesis between sin and creation. Put differently, the incarnation, passion, and resurrection in Jesus Christ means that his grace restores an original good creation. God's original thesis is reasserted and reestablished, but also, as John Paul II asserts in the above quote, enriched, fulfilled, and perfected. This redemption restores the very heart of human nature, causing the rebirth of the human self in Christ (Col. 2:13; 2 Cor. 5:17). "Christ alone, through his humanity, reveals the totality of the mystery of man…. The key to his self-understanding lies in contemplating the divine Prototype, the Word made flesh, the eternal Son of the Father." "Without the Gospel," John Paul adds, "man remains a dramatic question with no adequate answer. The correct response to the question about man is Christ, *Redemptor Hominis*."[117] This rebirth manifests itself in the integral redemption of the whole man in Christ through the fellowship of the Father, Son, and Holy Spirit, and with one another in them, which has been given to us in grace (Rom. 5:5). Indeed, this redemption in Christ becomes a vision of cosmic redemption for the whole creation, including

---

[117] John Paul II, *Memory and Identity*, 110, 114.

the life of culture. Indeed, God's grace in Christ *restores all life to its fullness, penetrating and perfecting and transforming the fallen creation from within its own order,* bringing creation into conformity with his will and purpose.[118]

---

[118] Portions of these three paragraphs were originally published in my article, "Living Truth for a Post-Christian World: The Message of Francis Schaeffer and Karol Wojtyla," *Religion & Liberty* 12, no. 6 (November/December 2002).

IV The *New Evangelization* of Culture[119]

"God is preparing a *great springtime for Christianity*," John Paul II proclaimed throughout his pontificate of almost twenty-seven years.[120] To prepare for that rich harvest, the people of God, the whole Church—especially the lay faithful, the Holy Father stresses—must be committed to the *new evangelization*. "The new evangelization that can make the twenty-first century a springtime of the Gospel is a task for the entire People of God, but will depend in a decisive way on the lay faithful being fully aware of their baptismal vocation and their responsibility for bringing the good news of Jesus Christ to their culture and society" (*SE*, 89).

If the new evangelization is to meet the challenge of this hour, the first and most urgent imperative is that the Church must remain true to her *evangelical* identity. As Paul VI wrote, "*Evangelization is the grace and vocation proper to the Church, her deepest identity. She exists in order to evangelize*, that is to say, in order to preach and teach, to be the channel of the gift of

---

[119] Portions of the concluding section of this essay were published in *John Paul II and the New Evangelization*, ed. Ralph Martin and Peter Williamson (Cincinnati: Servant Books, 2006), 288–95, 312–13.

[120] John Paul II, *Springtime of Evangelization*, The Complete Texts of the Holy Father's 1998 ad Limina Addresses to the Bishops of the United States, ed. and intro. Fr. Thomas D. Williams, L.C. (San Francisco: Ignatius Press, 1999), 38. Subsequent references to *SE* will be made parenthetically in the text.

grace, to reconcile sinners with God, and to perpetuate Christ's sacrifice in the Mass, which is the memorial of His death and glorious resurrection."[121] In other words, the Church will fulfill the task in which its deepest identity is based when it proclaims throughout the world "the full truth of the Gospel ... with renewed vigor '*Jesus Christ, the one Savior of the world, yesterday, today and for ever*'" (*SE*, 40, 42).

John Paul II called his Christ-centered approach to the transformation of culture, the *new evangelization*. Why does he call this evangelization *new*?

The reason that comes readily to mind in reference to Europe, but surely a similar point could be made about America, is because of: "*the loss of Europe's [and America's] Christian memory and heritage*, accompanied by a kind of practical agnosticism and religious indifference whereby many Europeans [and Americans] give the impression of living without spiritual roots and somewhat like heirs who have squandered a patrimony entrusted to them."[122] Significantly, there is also the "advance of secularism," which includes a relativistic attitude toward truth itself, in the flow of the culture and society, gradually changing cultural institutions such as marriage and family and broader societal structures such as mainstream media, political, legal, educational, and health care institutions. Furthermore, with the Christian faith under attack by this advancement, many Christians have *privatized* their faith, adopting a "citadel mentality," retreating behind the walls of the Church, and hoping that secularization will not reach them. Thus: "Many people are no longer able to integrate the Gospel message into their daily experience; living one's faith in Jesus becomes increasingly difficult in a social and cultural setting in which that faith is constantly challenged and threatened. In many social settings, it is easier

---

[121] Paul VI, *Evangelii Nuntiandi*, no. 14.

[122] John Paul II, *Ecclesia in Europa*, 2003 Post-Synodal Apostolic Exhortation, no. 7.

to be identified as an agnostic than a believer. The impression is given that unbelief is self-explanatory, whereas belief needs a sort of social legitimization which is neither obvious nor taken for granted." Alternatively, "European culture gives the impression of 'silent apostasy' on the part of people who have all that they need and who live as if God does not exist." In sum, John Paul adds, "*We are witnessing the emergence of a new culture ... whose content and character are often in conflict with the Gospel and the dignity of the human person.*" [123]

Western culture is failing because its Christian roots are eroding. This failing culture has reached its lowest point in the emerging *culture of death*, which is antithetical to what John Paul II also calls the *culture of life* in the 1995 encyclical *Evangelium Vitae.* There are four specific roots of the culture of death: individual autonomy; a debased notion of freedom detached from objective truth; the eclipse of the sense of God and, in consequence, of the human person; and the darkening of human conscience, indeed, moral blindness, resulting in a confusion between good and evil in the individual and in society.[124] In short, the Church is engaged in a battle for the soul of Western culture. What is the consequence of this conclusion for the Church? What ought *we* to do in engaging this failing culture?

In response, John Paul II has provided us with an all-embracive "plan of action" involving the whole Church in the whole spectrum of life and in the whole culture (*SE*, 59, 76).[125] We are called to be the people of God at the *service of life*. We need to bring the gospel of Jesus to the heart of every man and woman. There is a deep spiritual hunger in every human heart "for fullness of life and truth" (*SE*, 56). In no uncertain terms, Pope John Paul II boldly proclaims the truth of the gospel: "Jesus Christ is the answer to the question that

---

[123] John Paul II, *Ecclesia in Europa*, nos. 7, 9.
[124] John Paul II, *Evangelium Vitae*, nos. 19–24.
[125] John Paul II, *Evangelium Vitae*, nos. 78–101.

is every human life" (cf. *SE*, 44, 58, 85). *"No demand … is more urgent than the 'new evangelization' needed to satisfy the spiritual hunger of our times"* (*SE*, 148).

Most important for its overall approach to culture, however, the Church must include each one of the typical answers, but now only as aspects of its total approach, to the enduring question of how Christ relates to culture. The *culture* that embodies the *gospel of life* is *opposed* to the *culture of death*—abortion, infanticide, physician-assisted suicide, euthanasia, cloning, along with issues regarding bioethics, sexual ethics, marriage, and family life (cf. *SE*, 148–49). Christians are not only called to be *against* these practices but also to be agents of Christ-centered cultural *renewal*. The Church must evangelize, indeed, transform not only individuals but also cultural institutions and broader societal structures that support and promote the *gospel of life*. God's people are called to be in service to life by *building a new culture of human life.*

At the core of the new evangelization is the good news that *human life is a good, a gift of God*: Man is made in the image of God (Gen. 1:26), who is the crown of creation given dominion over all of creation (Gen. 1:28), possessing human dignity, and incomparable value. Man's image was marred by sin but is "restored, renewed, and brought to perfection" in and through the redemptive incarnation of the eternal Son of God, Jesus Christ. John Paul says: "All who commit themselves to following Christ are given the fullness of life … God's plan for human beings is this: that they should be 'conformed to the image of his Son' (Rom. 8:29)." Furthermore: "The dignity of [human] life is linked not only to its beginning, to the fact that it comes from God, but also to its final end, to its destiny of fellowship with God in knowledge and love of him." Thus, *"The Gospel of God's love for man, the Gospel of the dignity of the person and the Gospel of life are a single and indivisible Gospel."* [126]

---

[126] John Paul II, *Evangelium Vitae*, no. 2, but also, nos. 32–36, and 38.

In order to be fully equipped as God's people to be at the service of life this "single and indivisible Gospel" must be taught and lived from the outset in the life of the family. Indeed, the family has a decisive and irreplaceable role to play in building a culture of life. Children must be raised by their parents with the understanding that *procreation* is about receiving, not possessing, the divine *gift of human life*. Human life is not only a *gift*, however, it is also a *task*. That is, they must learn that in receiving this gift they have a corresponding responsibility to affirm and protect human life as a good. They do this by making choices that show respect for others, not only by respecting their rights, but also, indeed chiefly, by the sincere *gift of self* shown in being hospitable, in engaging in dialogue, in generous service, in bearing each others' burdens, and in expressing solidarity with others. At the root of this self-giving is the divine commandment *to love, respect, and promote life*, especially but not only where life is weak and defenseless but also where life is challenged by hardship, sickness or rejection, and suffering. "Human life is sacred and inviolable at every stage and in every situation; it is an indivisible good.[127]

The truths of this single and indivisible gospel of life must be taught thereafter "*in catechesis, in the various forms of preaching, in personal dialogue, and in all educational activity.*" Yet, there is more: the gospel of life should be culturally embodied. As John Paul II constantly urged, "A faith that does not become culture [that is, inculturated] is a faith not fully accepted, not entirely thought out, not faithfully lived."[128] To that end, we must support and express solidarity with agencies and centers of service to life such as hospitals, clinics, and convalescent homes by emphasizing the intrinsic and undeniable *moral dimension* of their responsibility. In particular, to be actively prolife for

---

[127] John Paul II, *Evangelium Vitae*, nos. 92–93, 96, and 52, 4, and for this quote at no. 87.

[128] John Paul II, cited in *Towards a Pastoral Approach to Culture*, no. 1.

the common good of society requires Christian health-care professionals—doctors, nurses, pharmacists, administrators, and chaplains—to bear witness to the gospel of life *in* their respective areas of responsibility. The apostolate of the laity "is exercised ... when they endeavor to have the Gospel spirit permeate and improve the temporal order, going about it in a way that bears clear witness to Christ and helps forward the salvation of men. Characteristic of the lay state is a life led in the midst of the world and of secular affairs, and hence laymen are called by God to make of their apostolate, through the vigor of their Christian spirit, a leaven in the world."[129] This apostolate is particularly important today given the current temptation of health-care professionals "to become manipulators of life, or even agents of death." This temptation may be resisted by recovering the meaning of the *Hippocratic Oath*, "which requires every doctor to commit himself to absolute respect for human life and its sacredness."[130]

Furthermore, Christians involved in the political, social, and civic arenas of cultural life are also responsible for implementing the gospel of life by "shaping society and developing cultural, economic, political, and legislative projects that, with respect for all and in keeping with democratic principles will contribute to the building of a society in which the dignity of each person is recognized and protected and the lives of all are defended and enhanced."[131] Moreover, Christian scholars—philosophers, theologians, indeed all those intellectuals engaged in the study of man—at work in institutions of higher education, centers, institutes, and committees addressing bio-ethical questions are also obligated by virtue of their calling in Christ to contribute to building a new culture of life.

At the start of this study, I referred to the central role that natural law plays in Catholic social teaching. What is the place of the natural law in building a new culture of life? This moral

---

[129] Vatican II, *Apostolicam Actuositatem*, no. 2.

[130] John Paul II, *Evangelium Vitae*, nos. 88–89.

[131] John Paul II, *Evangelium Vitae*, no. 90.

law not only grounds human dignity in a source of truth and morality outside the state itself, but it also leads to the rejection of the absolute state, subordinating the latter's power to the rule of law. Furthermore, the natural law, given its moral objectivity, leads to the rejection of a democracy that is based on the absolutization of the majority principle. As Benedict XVI correctly argues, "The majority cannot be an ultimate principle, since there are values that no majority is entitled to annul. It can never be right to kill innocent persons, and no power can make this legitimate."[132] Elsewhere, Benedict writes, "But majorities, too, can be blind or unjust, as history teaches us very plainly.... The majority principle always leaves open the question of the ethical foundations of law. This is the question of whether there is something that can never become law but always remains injustice [remains wrong]; or, to reverse this formulation, whether there is something that is of its very nature inalienably law, something that is antecedent to every majority decision and must be respected by all such decisions."[133] Who would disagree? The brief answer to this question here must be: those who lack confidence in the truth-attaining capacities of human reason. Such a lack signifies, according to Benedict XVI, "*a crisis of political reason, which is a crisis of politics as such.*" We come thus to the nub of the issue before us. Both Benedict and John Paul II are persuaded that what is ultimately at stake in an authentic democracy is the "defense of reason." "Reason," adds Benedict, "that is,

---

[132] Joseph Cardinal Ratzinger, "To Change or to Preserve? Political Visions and Political Praxis," in *Values in a Time of Upheaval*, trans. Brian McNeil, C.R.V. (New York: Crossroad, 2006), 11–29, and for this quote, 27.

[133] Ratzinger, "What Keeps the World Together, The Pre-political Moral Foundations of a Free State," in *Values in a Time of Upheaval*, 31–44, and for this quote, 34. There is another translation of this same essay available in Joseph Cardinal Ratzinger (Pope Benedict XVI) and Jürgen Habermas, *Dialectics of Secularization: On Reason and Religion*, ed. with foreword Florian Schuller, trans. Brian McNeil, C.R.V. (San Francisco: Ignatius Press, 2006), 53–80, and for this quote, 60. It is the translation from this book that I am citing in the text.

moral reason is above the majority." "But how is it possible to discern these ultimate values that are the basis of all 'rational' and morally correct politics and are therefore binding on every person, irrespective of how majorities may shift and change? What are these values?"[134]

In reply to the question in the concluding sentence of this passage, here is a summary statement of these core values:

> In the face of *fundamental and inalienable ethical demands*, Christian must recognize that what is at stake is the essence of the moral law, which concerns the integral good of the human person. This is the case with laws concerning *abortion* and euthanasia.... Such laws must defend the basic right to life from conception to natural death. In the same way, it is necessary to recall the duty to respect and protect the rights of the *human embryo*. Analogously, the *family* needs to be safeguarded and promoted, based on monogamous marriage between a man and a woman, and protected in its unity and stability in the face of modern laws on divorce: in no way can other forms of cohabitation be placed on the same level as marriage, nor can they receive legal recognition as such. The same is true for the freedom of parents regarding the *education* of their children; it is an inalienable right recognized also by the Universal Declaration on Human Rights.... In addition, there is the right to *religious freedom* and the development of an *economy* that is at the service of the human person and of the common good, with respect for social justice, the principles of human solidarity and subsidiarity.[135]

I would add here that John Paul II and Benedict XVI are persuaded that, in the former's words, "authentic democracy is possible only in a State ruled by law, and on the basis of a

---

[134] Ratzinger, "To Change or to Preserve?" 27.

[135] Ratzinger, "Doctrinal Note on Some Questions Regarding the Participation of Catholics in Political Life," Congregation for the Doctrine of the Faith, November 24, 2002, no. 4, http://www.vatican.va/roman_curia/congregations/cfaith/documents/rc_con_cfaith_doc_20.

correct concept of the human person" (*CA*, no. 46). Hence, they both argue against the thesis that "the modern concept of democracy [is] indissolubly linked to that of relativism" (as Benedict puts it).[136] John Paul elaborates: "Nowadays there is a tendency to claim that agnosticism and skeptical relativism are the philosophy and the basic attitude which correspond to democratic forms of life. Those who are convinced that they know the truth and firmly adhere to it are considered unreliable from a democratic point of view, since they do not accept that truth is determined by the majority, or that it is subject to variation according to different political trends" (*CA*, no. 46). What started out as a mere recognition of the fact of moral and religious diversity, and hence disagreement, in contemporary society has turned into the stronger epistemological claim that excludes the recognition of moral and religious truth claims. If we cannot be sure of the truth, or if truth is culturally, socially, and individually relative, that is, nothing but a matter of inter-pretation and perspective, then everyone's freedom is best protected from manipulation, coercion, and deception—so the argument goes. In response to this argument, John Paul observes in this regard, "if there is no ultimate truth to guide and direct political activity, then ideas and convictions can easily be manipulated for reasons of power" (*CA*, no. 46). Indeed, agnosticism and skeptical relativism about truth do not protect human freedom and hence the dignity of the human person. The very opposite is true, according to both popes. In a world without truth in the objective sense, might makes right. Without transcendent truth, which provides a foundation for human rights and basic freedoms, we actually open the door to totalitarianism, and man is vulnerable to the violence of manipulation, coercion, and deception. In short, argues John Paul, the dignity of the human person cannot

---

[136] Ratzinger, "*What Is Truth?* The Significance of Religious and Ethical Values in a Pluralistic Society," in *Values in a Time of Upheaval*, 53–72, and for this quote, 55.

be inviolable unless it is objectively grounded in truth about human nature. "If there is no transcendent truth, in obedience to which man achieves his full identity, then there is no sure principle for guaranteeing just relations between people.... Thus, the root of modern totalitarianism is to be found in the denial of the transcendent dignity of the human person who, as the visible image of the invisible God, is therefore by his very nature the subject of rights which no one may violate—no individual, group, class, nation or State" (*CA*, no. 44). What rights is the pope talking about?

> Among the most important of these rights, mention must be made of the right to life, an integral part of which is the right of the child to develop in the mother's womb from the moment of conception; the right to live in a united family and in a moral environment conducive to the growth of the child's personality; the right to develop one's intelligence and freedom in seeking and knowing the truth; the right to share in the work which makes wise use of the earth's material resources, and to derive from that work the means to support oneself and one's dependents; and the right freely to establish a family, to have and to rear children through the responsible exercise of one's sexuality. In a certain sense, the source and synthesis of these rights is religious freedom, understood as the right to live in the truth of one's faith and in conformity with one's transcendent dignity as a person (*CA*, no. 47).

In speaking of modern totalitarianism, we should understand that John Paul is thinking here not only of national socialism and the Marxist-Leninism of the twentieth century, but also, indeed chiefly, of the "thinly disguised totalitarianism" of a "democracy without [absolute] values" (*CA*, no. 46). Although the pope does not explicitly say so, we can safely surmise that he means here the thinly disguised totalitarianism of a secularist political liberalism that moves religion or a religiously based morality into the private sphere, appearing to take up a neutral position on religion, but holding that it should not be invoked in matters of public policy, indeed, should not even be given public recognition. Put differently, given the fact of diversity in our society on moral and religious matters, making and assessing truth claims regarding such matters is out of bounds in public life—or so we are regularly told. "Truth is controversial." "The concept of 'truth' has in fact," adds Benedict, "moved into the zone of antidemocratic intolerance. It is not now a public good, but something private.... [I]t is not the truth of society as a whole."[137] Religion and public life are therefore compartmentalized in the name of liberal values such as tolerance and diversity. "The question must be asked," however, "whether all this is as fair as it appears." As Roger Trigg rightly observes,

> It may seem tolerant to take up a neutral position on religion, but excluding any agreement involving religion is far from neutral. Many religious believers will be excluded from public debate as their beliefs are ruled a private matter.... When, however, an issue like abortion is fought over, the exclusion of religious grounds will only leave religious believers disgruntled and feeling that their voice has not been heard. They have not even been overruled. They have not been listened to.... It is not clear why someone who believes on religious grounds that a human fetus is a person should be excluded from the debate while a non-believer is under no such restraint and is free to argue that the fetus is not a person.[138]

We reach here the crux of John Paul's charge that the specter of a thinly disguised totalitarianism looms large in a democracy that is intolerant toward moral and religious truth claims. He is drawing our attention to a secularist totalitarianism whose

---

[137] Ratzinger, "*What Is Truth?* The Significance of Religious and Ethical Values in a Pluralistic Society," 55.

[138] Roger Trigg, *Rationality and Religion* (Oxford: Blackwell, 1998), 16.

perspective often goes undetected. This form of totalitarianism—secular political liberalism—is therefore far from neutral.[139]

Thus, the moral truth regarding the intrinsic goodness and inviolability of human life is a fundamental value for all human beings, indeed for the common good of the whole of human society, and hence is indispensable to democracy. Furthermore, moral knowledge of this good can be had by the light of human reason.

> The *Gospel of life* is not for believers alone: *It is for everyone.* The issue of life and its defense and promotion is not a concern of Christians alone. Although faith provides special insight and strength, this question arises in every human conscience which seeks the truth and which cares about the future of humanity. Life certainly has a sacred and religious value, but in no way is that value a concern only of believers. *The value at stake is one which every human being can grasp by the light of reason; thus it necessarily concerns everyone.*"[140]

Christians should therefore form alliances with all men of good will and sound judgment who share a commitment to the sanctity of human life, unconditionally respecting "the right to life of every innocent person—from concept to natural death—[as] one of the pillars on which every civil society stands."[141] What is more, they should communicate this commitment and other moral principles on the field of rational debate, in the public square, dispelling the misconception that prolife principles are a matter of *pure faith* rather than rationally grounded beliefs about human nature. In the words of Princeton professor and

---

[139] On this point, see also Nicholas Wolterstorff, "The Role of Religion in Decision and Discussion of Political Issues," in *Religion in the Public Square: The Place of Religious Convictions in Political Debate*, ed. Robert Audi and Nicholas Wolterstorff (New York: Rowman & Littlefield, 1997), 67–120, esp. 105.

[140] John Paul II, *Evangelium Vitae*, no. 101; italics added to the last sentence.

[141] John Paul II, *Evangelium Vitae*, no. 101.

author Robert P. George, "These principles are available for rational affirmation by people of good will and sound judgment, even apart from their revelation by God in the Scriptures and in the life, death, and resurrection of Christ."[142]

Of course presupposed here by Robert George and John Paul II is an understanding of the relationship between faith and reason and hence of the role of religion in public life that is not generally accepted, indeed, is controversial. Why should not religious and moral truth claims be publicly recognized? In particular, does the Christian faith have no public role to play? At issue here is not a political theocracy. "*Christian truth* is not of this kind." "In constantly reaffirming the transcendent dignity of the person," adds John Paul, "the Church's method is always that of respect for freedom" (*CA*, no. 46). That is, the freedom to choose reason over coercion, argument over force. Indeed, as Roger Trigg rightly notes, "freedom may be seen as the precondition of rationality."[143] Significantly, says John Paul, "freedom attains its full development only by accepting the truth." Here again the pope emphasizes his critique of a so-called post-truth democracy (to borrow a phrase from Jürgen Habermas):[144]

> In a world without truth, freedom loses its foundation and man is exposed to the violence of passion and to manipulation, both open and hidden. The Christian upholds freedom and serves it, constantly offering to others the truth which he has known (cf. John 8:31–32), in accordance with the missionary nature of his vocation. While paying heed to every fragment of truth which he encounters in the life experience and in the

---

[142] Robert P. George, *The Clash of Orthodoxies: Law, Religion, and Morality in Crisis* (Wilmington, Del.: ISI Books, 2001), 7.

[143] Roger Trigg, *Rationality and Religion*, 26.

[144] Jürgen Habermas, "Religion in the Public Sphere" (public lecture, University of San Diego, March 4, 2005), http://www.sandiego.edu/pdf/pdf_library/habermaslecture031105_c939cceb2ab087bdfc6df291ec0fc3fa.pdf.

> culture of individuals and of nations, he will not fail to affirm in dialogue with others all that his faith and the correct use of reason have enabled him to understand. (*CA*, no. 46)

I should like then to summarize in three theses the principles informing the Christian's role in public life:

1. The Christian should reject the pernicious error of compartmentalizing his faith and life. Rather, given the integral role that the Christian faith should play in his entire life, the Christian should affirm and thus display "the unity of Christian life: coherence between faith and life, Gospel and culture, as recalled by the Second Vatican Council."[145] This is not only a Catholic principle but also a Reformed one. "It belongs to the *religious convictions* of a good many religious people in our society that *they ought to base* their decisions concerning issues of justice *on* their religious convictions. They do not view it as an option whether or not to do so. It is their conviction that they ought to strive for wholeness, integrity, integration, in their lives."[146]

2. The Christian should affirm the principle regarding the necessary correlation between reason and faith, reason and revelation, as sources of knowledge serving as checks on one another. "They need each other, and they must acknowledge one another's validity."[147] Benedict XVI applies this principle to the context in which we live today where, he says, "there exist pathologies of religion, as well as pathologies

---

[145] "Doctrinal Note on Some Questions Regarding the Participation of Catholics in Political Life," Congregation for the Doctrine of the Faith, 2002, no. 9. In *Gaudium et spes*, the Council Fathers spoke of "the dichotomy between the faith which many profess and the practice of their daily lives" as "pernicious" (no. 43).

[146] Wolterstorff, "The Role of Religion in Decision and Discussion of Political Issues," 105.

[147] Ratzinger, "What Keeps the World Together, The Pre-political Moral Foundations of a Free State," 43.

of reason."[148] He adds, "Religion must continually accept the purification and regulation that reason carries out.... [R]eason too must be admonished to keep to its own boundaries and to learn to listen to what the great religious traditions of mankind have to say. If reason becomes fully emancipated and lays aside this willingness to learn, this correlation [of reason] with religion, it takes on a destructive character."[149]

---

[148] Ratzinger, "Searching for Peace, Tensions and Dangers," in *Values in a Time of Upheaval*, 101–16, and for this quote, 108–9.

[149] Ratzinger, "What Keeps the World Together, The Pre-political Moral Foundations of a Free State," 42–43. For some examples of these pathologies, see "Searching for Peace, Tensions and Dangers," in *Values in a Time of Upheaval*, 109–10. On religion:

> God or the divine can turn into the absolutization of one's own power and one's own interests.... This is made even worse by the fact that the intention to act on behalf of one's cause is charged with a fanaticism centered on the absolute, a religious fanaticism, and thus becomes completely brutal and blind. God has become an idol in which human beings adore their own will. We see this in the terrorists' ideology of martyrdom.... Sects in the Western worlds also provide examples of an irrationality and a perversion of religion that show how dangerous religion becomes when it loses its orientation.

On reason: "But there also exists a pathology of reason that is completely detached from God, as we have seen in the totalitarian ideologies that parted company with God and wanted to construct the new man, the new world." Benedict gives as examples here Hitler, Marxism, and Pol Pot, but also refers to Western intellectual developments.

> Was not the atomic bomb already a transgression of boundaries, where reason refused to be a constructive force but instead sought its strength in the ability to destroy? Now that reason is reaching for the very roots of life in its investigation of the genetic code, there is an increasing tendency to stop seeing man as a gift of the Creator (or of "nature") and to make him a product. Man is "made," and what one can "make" one can also unmake. Human dignity dissolves. And where are we then to find an anchor for human rights? How is respect for man—even the one who is conquered, weak, suffering, or handicapped—to survive?

3. This basic principle should guide the discussions in public life between the religious and secular citizens of a democratic community. Both citizens must be willing to reason about what is true, that is, to enter seriously and engage in a discussion on moral and religious truth claims. But I believe that this will happen only if both sides "have cognitive reasons to take seriously each other's contributions to controversial subjects in the public debate."[150] In keeping with the principle regarding the necessary correlation between reason and faith, on the one hand, the Christian citizen can take seriously the contributions of fellow citizens who are secular. On the other hand, the secular citizen who has a secularist consciousness lacks the correct epistemic attitude to his fellow citizens who are religious because he presumes that religion makes no cognitive claims. Consequently, I think that secular citizens should engage in a "self-critical assessment of the limits of secular reason," as Habermas puts it, "rejecting a narrow scientistic concept of reason and the exclusion of religious doctrines from the genealogy of reason."[151] This recommendation by agnostic Habermas is remarkably similar to Benedict's own analysis. He, too, rejects a "reason [that] reduces itself to those things that are open to experimental examination." The result of this reductionist notion of reason is, he says, to banish all morality and religion "to the sphere of the 'subjective,' and this entire sphere has nothing to do with shared reason. Religion and morality do not fall within the province of reason; there are no longer any 'objective' shared criteria of morality."[152]

---

[150] Jürgen Habermas, "Pre-political Foundations of the Democratic Constitutional State," in *Dialectics of Secularization*, 19–52, and for this quite, 47.

[151] Habermas, "Religion in the Public Sphere."

[152] Ratzinger, "Searching for Peace," 110.

By contrast, Benedict's proposal for restoring faith in reason's truth-attaining capacities goes further than Habermas. The Christian holds that "faith in God who is Logos is at the same time faith in the creative power of reason." "God is Logos—meaning, reason, and word, and that is why man corresponds to God when his reason is open and he pleads the cause of a reason that is not allowed to be blind to the moral dimensions of existence." "But," he adds, "a reason that completely detaches itself from God, and is willing to accept his existence only in the realm of the subjective, loses its orientation, thereby opening the door to the powers of destruction." Indeed, such a concept of reason is sick. "Sick reason ultimately regards as fundamentalism all knowledge of definitively valid values and every insistence that reason is capable of discerning truth." Sick reason "paralyzes and destroys itself."[153]

Of course, the Christian citizen should urge the secular citizen to notice that not only does the biblical revelation about faith in the God who is Logos ground our understanding of the dignity of human reason, but this revelation also, indeed chiefly, discloses the whole truth that human dignity is revealed in Jesus Christ, God truly become man. In other words, "When he presents the heart of his redemptive mission, Jesus says: 'I came that they may have life, and have it abundantly' (John 10:10). In truth, he is referring to that 'new' and 'eternal' life which consists in communion with the father, to which every person is freely called in the Son by the power of the Sanctifying Spirit. It is precisely in this 'life' that all the aspects and stages of human life achieve their full significance."[154] In a nutshell, this is the *leitmotif* of John Paul II's call

---

[153] Ratzinger, "Searching for Peace," 111.
[154] John Paul II, *Evangelium Vitae*, no. 1.

for the *new evangelization*, echoing Vatican II: "In reality it is only in the mystery of the Word made flesh that the mystery of man truly becomes clear" (*GS*, no. 22), which is to say that there is no true self-knowledge apart from Jesus Christ.

Pope John Paul II summed up the call:

> Indeed, the Church's mission of spreading the Gospel not only demands that the Good News be preached ever more widely and to ever greater numbers of men and women, but [also] that the very power of the Gospel should permeate thought patterns, standards of judgment, and the norms of behavior; in a word, it is necessary that the whole of human culture be steeped in the Gospel. The cultural atmosphere in which a human being lives has a great influence upon his or her way of thinking and, thus, of acting. Therefore, a division between faith and culture is more than a small impediment to evangelization, while a culture penetrated with the Christian spirit is an instrument that favors the spreading of the Good News.[155]

This last point makes clear the intrinsic connection between the new evangelization and the cultural mandate, namely, a commitment to the new evangelization entails a commitment to the renewal of culture, indeed, the whole spectrum of life. This renewal is ongoing because it is caught in the eschatological tension between the present (the now) and future (not yet) dimensions of the kingdom of God until its culminating fullness at the end of time.

---

[155] John Paul II, "A Deep Commitment to Authentic Christian Living," *The Whole Truth about Man*, ed. with intro. James V. Schall, S.J. (Boston: St. Paul Editions, 1981), 84–91, and for this citation, 89.

References

Church Documents

Catechism of the Catholic Church. 1994. Revised 2000.

Compendium of the Social Doctrine of the Church. Pontifical Council for Justice and Peace. 2005.

Dei Filius (*Dogmatic Constitution on the Catholic Faith*). First Vatican Council. 1870.

"Doctrinal Note on Some Questions Regarding the Participation of Catholics in Political Life." Congregation for the Doctrine of the Faith, 2002. www.vatican.va/roman_curia/congregations/cfaith/documents/rc_con_cfaith_doc_20.

Gaudium et Spes *(Pastoral Constitution on the Church in the Modern World).* Second Vatican Council. 1964.

Lumen Gentium (*Dogmatic Constitution on the Church*). Second Vatican Council. 1964.

Pope John Paul II. Post-Synodal Apostolic Exhortation *Ecclesia in Europe.* 2003.

———. Encyclical Letter *Fides et Ratio.* 1998.

———. Encyclical Letter *Evangelium Vitae.* 1995.

———. Post-Synodal Apostolic Exhortation *Ecclesia in Africa.* 1995.

———. Apostolic Letter *Tertio Millennio Adveniente.* 1994.

———. Encyclical Letter *Centesimus Annus.* 1991.

―――. Encyclical Letter *Dominum et Vivificantem*. 1986.

Pope Paul VI. Apostolic Exhortation *Evangelii Nuntiandi*. 1975.

Towards a Pastoral Approach to Culture. Pontifical Council for Culture. 1999.

Books and Articles

Aquinas, St. Thomas. *Commentary on the* De Trinitate *of Boethius*. Translated with introduction and notes by Armand Maurer. Toronto: Pontifical Institute of Medieval Studies, 1987.

―――. *Summa Theologiae*.

Balthasar, Hans Urs von. "On the Tasks of Catholic Philosophy in Our Time." *Communio: International Catholic Review* 20 (Spring 1993): 147–87.

―――. *Love Alone*. New York: Sheed and Ward, 1969.

―――. *The Theology of Karl Barth*. San Francisco: Ignatius Press, 1992.

Bavinck, Herman. "Common Grace." Translated by R. C. van Leeuwen. *Calvin Theological Journal* 24, no. 1 (1989): 35–65.

―――. *Reformed Dogmatics*. Vol. 1, *Prolegomena*. Edited by John Bolt. Translated by John Vriend. Grand Rapids: Baker Academic, 2003 (1895).

Beabout, Gregory R., and Eduardo J. Echeverria. "The Culture of Consumerism: A Catholic and Personalist Critique." *Journal of Markets & Morality* 5, no. 2 (Fall 2002): 339–83.

Berkouwer, G. C. *General Revelation*. Grand Rapids: Eerdmans, 1955.

Budziszewski, J. *Evangelicals in the Public Square*. Grand Rapids: Baker Academic, 2006.

Calvin, John. *Institutes of the Christian Religion*. Edited by John T. McNeill. Philadelphia: Westminster, 1960.

Concise Dictionary of Theology, A. Edited by Gerald O'Collins, S.J. and Edward G. Farrugia, S.J. New York: Paulist Press, 1991.

De Lubac, Henri. *A Brief Catechesis on Nature and Grace*. Translated by Richard Arnandez, F.S.C. San Francisco: Ignatius Press, 1984.

————. *Catholicism: Christ and the Common Destiny of Man.* Translated by Lancelot C. Sheppard and Sister Elizabeth Englund, O.C.D. San Francisco: Ignatius Press, 1988 (1938).

————. *The Mystery of the Supernatural.* Translated by Rosemary Sheed. New York: Crossroad, 1998 (1965).

————. *Theological Fragments.* San Francisco: Ignatius Press, 1989.

Dolan, Jay. *In Search of an American Catholicism.* Oxford: Oxford University Press, 2002.

Dooyeweerd, Herman. *A New Critique of Theoretical Thought.* Translated by David H. Freeman and H. de Jongste. Philadelphia: Presbyterian & Reformed, 1955 (1936).

————. *In the Twilight of Western Thought: Studies in the Pretended Autonomy of Philosophical Thought.* Nutley, N.J.: Craig Press, 1968.

Echeverria, Eduardo. "Living Truth for a Post-Christian World: The Message of Francis Schaeffer and Karol Wojtyla." *Religion & Liberty* 12, no. 6 (November/December 2002).

————. "Nature and Grace: The Theological Foundations of Jacques Maritain's Public Philosophy," *Journal of Markets & Morality* 4, no. 2 (2001): 240–68.

Gay, Craig M. "Consumerism." In *The Complete Book of Everyday Christianity: An A-to-Z Guide to Following Christ in Every Aspect of Life.* Edited by Robert Banks and R. Paul Stevens. Downers Grove, Ill.: InterVarsity Press, 1997.

George, Francis Cardinal. "A New Apologetics for a New Evangelization," *Theology Digest* 47, no. 4 (Winter 2000): 341–59.

————. "Catholic Faith and the Secular Academy." *Logos* 4, no. 4 (Fall 2001): 73–81.

————. "Law and Culture," *Ave Maria Law Review* 1, no. 1 (Spring 2003): 1–17.

————. "One Lord and One Church for One World," *Origins* 30, no. 34 (February 8, 2001): 541–49.

————. "Public Morality in a Global Society: Catholics and Muslims in Dialogue," *Theology Digest* 49, no. 4 (Winter 2002): 319–33.

————. "The Culture in Which We Evangelize." Paper presented at Sacred Heart Major Seminary, St. John Conference Center, Plymouth, Mich., March 24–26, 2006.

————. "The Promotion of Missiological Studies in Seminaries," www.sedos.org/english/george_e.htm.

George, Robert P. *The Clash of Orthodoxies: Law, Religion, and Morality in Crisis*. Wilmington, Del.: ISI Books, 2001.

Gilson, Etienne. *The Philosopher and Theology*. Translated by Ralph MacDonald, C.S.B. London: Sheed & Ward, 1939.

Grabill, Stephen J. *Rediscovering the Natural Law in Reformed Theological Ethics*. Grand Rapids: Eerdmans, 2006.

Grisez, Germain. *The Way of the Lord Jesus*. Vol. 1, *Christian Moral Principles*. Quincy, Ill.: Franciscan Press, 1983.

Guardini, Romano. *The End of the Modern World*. Wilmington, Del.: ISI Books, 2001 (1950).

Guarino, Thomas G. *Foundations of Systematic Theology*. New York: T&T Clark, 2005.

Gustafson, James M. "Theological Bases." In *Protestant and Roman Catholic Ethics*. Chicago: University of Chicago Press, 1978.

Habermas, Jürgen. "Religion in the Public Sphere." Public lecture, University of San Diego, March 4, 2005), www.sandiego.edu/pdf/pdf_library/habermaslecture031105_c939cceb2ab087bdfc6df291ec0fc3fa.pdf.

Harvey, Van A. "The Pathos of Liberal Theology." *Journal of Religion* 56 (1976): 382–91.

Heslam, Peter S. *Creating a Christian Worldview: Abraham Kuyper's Lectures on Calvinism*. Grand Rapids: Eerdmans, 1998.

Hittinger, Russell. *The First Grace: Rediscovering the Natural Law in a Post-Christian World*. Wilmington, Del.: ISI Books, 2003.

Hoitenga, Dewey J., Jr., *John Calvin and the Will: A Critique and Corrective*. Grand Rapids: Baker, 1997.

Hughes, W. D., O.P., "The Infusion of Virtues (Appendix 3)." In *Summa Theologiae*, vol. 23, *Virtue* by St. Thomas Aquinas. New York: McGraw-Hill, 1975.

International Theological Commission. "Faith and Inculturation." In *Catholicism and Secularization in America*. Edited by David L. Schindler. Huntington, Ind.: Our Sunday Visitor, 1990.

John Paul II, Pope. "A Deep Commitment to Authentic Christian Living." In *The Whole Truth about Man*. Edited with introduction by James V. Schall, S.J. Boston: St. Paul Editions, 1981.

———. "Dialogue between Cultures for a Civilization of Love and Peace." *Origins* 30, no. 8 (January 4, 2001).

———. *John Paul II and the New Evangelization*. Edited by Ralph Martin and Peter Williamson. Cincinnati: Servant Books, 2006.

———. *Memory and Identity, Conversations at the Dawn of a Millennium*. New York: Rizzoli, 2005.

———. *Springtime of Evangelization: The Complete Texts of the Holy Father's 1998 ad Limina Addresses to the Bishops of the United States*. Edited and introduction by Fr. Thomas D. Williams, L.C. San Francisco: Ignatius Press, 1999.

John XXIII, Pope. "Allocutio habita d. 11 oct. 1962, in initio Concilii," *Acta Apostolicae Sedis* vol. 54 (1962): 796.

Kuyper, Abraham. "Common Grace." In *Abraham Kuyper: A Centennial Reader*, 165–201. Edited by James D. Bratt. Grand Rapids: Eerdmans, 1998.

———. *De Gemeene Gratie (Common Grace)*, 3 vols. Amsterdam: Höveker & Wormser, 1902–1904.

———. *Lectures on Calvinism*. Grand Rapids: Eerdmans, 1931.

Lonergan, Bernard, S.J., *Method in Theology*. New York: Herder and Herder, 1972.

MacIntyre, Alasdair. "The Fate of Theism." In *The Religious Significance of Atheism*. New York: Columbia University, 1969.

Maritain, Jacques. "The Conquest of Freedom." In *The Education of Man: The Educational Philosophy of Jacques Maritain*. Edited by Donald and Idella Gallagher. Garden City, N.Y.: Doubleday, 1962.

———. *Integral Humanism: Temporal and Spiritual Problems of a New Christendom*. Translated by Joseph Evans. 1936. Reprint. New York: Scribner's, 1968.

————. *On the Philosophy of History*. Edited by Joseph W. Evans. New York: Scribner's, 1957.

McGreevy, John T. *Catholicism and American Freedom: A History*. New York: W. W. Norton, 2003.

Mouw, Richard J. *He Shines in All That's Fair: Culture and Common Grace*. Grand Rapids: Eerdmans, 2001.

Murray, John Courtney, S.J., *We Hold These Truths: Catholic Reflections on the American Proposition*. New York: Sheed and Ward, 1960.

Newman, John Henry Cardinal. *An Essay on the Development of Christian Doctrine*, 6th ed. 1845. Reprint. Notre Dame: University of Notre Dame Press, 1989.

Nichols, Aidan, O.P. "Rerelating Faith and Culture." In *Christendom Awake: On Reenergizing the Church in Culture*. Grand Rapids: Eerdmans, 1999.

————. *Epiphany: A Theological Introduction to Catholicism*. Collegeville, Minn.: Liturgical Press, 1996.

————. "Integral Evangelization." *Josephinum Journal of Theology* 13, no. 1 (2006): 66–80.

Niebuhr, H. Richard. *Christ and Culture*. New York: Harper & Row, 1951.

Pelikan, Jaroslav "Nature and Grace." In *The Christian Tradition: A History of the Development of Doctrine*. Vol. 1, *The Emergence of the Catholic Tradition (100–600)*. Chicago: University of Chicago Press, 1971.

Pope Benedict XVI. "Communication and Culture." In *On the Way to Jesus Christ*. Translated by Michael J. Miller. San Francisco: Ignatius Press, 2005.

Rahner, Karl. *Nature and Grace and Other Essays*. Translated by Dinah Wharton. New York: Sheed and Ward, 1963.

Ratzinger, Joseph Cardinal, and Jürgen Habermas, *Dialectics of Secularization: On Reason and Religion*. Edited with foreword by Florian Schuller. Translated by Brian McNeil, C.R.V. San Francisco: Ignatius Press, 2006.

Ratzinger, Joseph Cardinal. *Truth and Tolerance: Christian Belief and World Religions*. Translated by Henry Taylor. San Francisco: Ignatius Press, 2003.

———. *Values in a Time of Upheaval.* Translated by Brian McNeil, C.R.V. New York: Crossroad, 2006.

Rowland, Tracey. *Culture and the Thomist Tradition after Vatican II.* New York: Routledge, 2003.

Schaeffer, Francis A. *The God Who Is There,* 30th anniversary edition. Downers Grove, Ill.: InterVarsity Press, 1998.

Schilder, Klaas. *Christ and Culture.* Translated by G. van Rongen and W. Helder. 1932. Reprint. Winnipeg: Premier, 1977.

Schindler, David L. "Christology, Public Theology, and Thomism: de Lubac, Balthasar, and Murray." In *The Future of Thomism.* Edited by Deal W. Hudson and Dennis William Moran. Minneapolis: American Maritain Association, 1992.

Seerveld, Calvin. *A Christian Critique of Art and Literature.* Ontario: Association for Reformed Scientific Studies, 1964.

Sharkey, Michael, ed. "Select Themes of Ecclesiology on the Occasion of the Eighth Anniversary of the Closing of the Second Vatican Council." In *International Theological Commission: Texts and Documents 1969–1985.* San Francisco: Ignatius Press, 1989.

Stob, Henry. "Calvin and Aquinas." In *Theological Reflections: Essays on Related Themes.* Grand Rapids: Eerdmans, 1981.

———. "Observations on the Concept of the Antithesis." In *Perspectives on the Christian Reformed Church: Studies in Its History, Theology, and Ecumenicity.* Edited by Peter De Klerk and Richard R. De Ridder. Grand Rapids: Baker, 1983.

Stout, Jeffrey. "The Voice of Theology in Contemporary Culture." In *Religion and America: Spirituality in a Secular Age.* Edited by Mary Douglas and Steven M. Tipton. Boston: Beacon Press, 1983.

Taylor, Charles. "Two Theories of Modernity." *Hastings Center Report* 25, no. 2 (March-April 1995): 24–33.

Trigg, Roger. *Rationality and Religion.* Oxford: Blackwell, 1998.

Van Til, Henry R. *The Calvinistic Concept of Culture.* 1951. Reprint. Grand Rapids: Baker Academic, 2001.

Wolters, Albert. "What Is To BeDone? Toward a Neo-Calvinist Agenda," www.wrf.ca/comment/article.cfm?ID=142.

Wolterstorff, Nicholas. "Keeping Faith: Talks for the New Faculty at Calvin College," *Occasional Papers from Calvin College* 7, no. 1 (February 1989).

———. "Tertullian's Enduring Question." *The Cresset* (June/July 1999).

———, and Robert Audi, eds. "The Role of Religion in Decision and Discussion of Political Issues." In *Religion in the Public Square: The Place of Religious Convictions in Political Debate*. New York: Rowman & Littlefield, 1997.

———. *Until Justice and Peace Embrace*. Grand Rapids: Eerdmans, 1983.

Zuidema, S. U. "Common Grace and Christian Action in Abraham Kuyper." In *Communication and Confrontation: A Philosophical Appraisal and Critique of Modern Society and Contemporary Thought*. Toronto: Wedge, 1972.

About the Author

EDUARDO J. ECHEVERRIA is Professor of Philosophy at Sacred Heart Major Seminary, Detroit, Michigan. He has advanced degrees in philosophy and theology and received his Ph.D. in philosophy from the Free University of Amsterdam in 1981. He has published articles in professional journals such as the *Thomist*, *Logos*, *Philosophia Reformata*, the *Journal of Markets and Morality*, and *Revista Portuguesa de Filosofia*.